THIS
WAS
SAWMILLING

This Was Sawmilling
by
Ralph W. Andrews

(opposite) **SCHOONER IN PACIFIC "DOG HOLE"** loading red-wood lumber by chute from mill on California cliff. Schooners could anchor in these holes only when weather and sea were comparatively calm. They swung twenty or thirty feet with tides and when beneath end of chute, clapperman released brake on stick of lumber and dropped it on deck. Captain "Midnight" Olson was a famous dare-devil skipper in this trade. (Photo Union Lumber Co. Collection)

4880 Lower Valley Road, Atglen, PA 19310 USA

Schiffer Books are available at special discounts for bulk purchases for sales promotions or premiums. Special editions, including personalized covers, corporate imprints, and excerpts can be created in large quantities for special needs. For more information contact the publisher:

Published by Schiffer Publishing Ltd.
4880 Lower Valley Road
Atglen, PA 19310
Phone: (610) 593-1777; Fax: (610) 593-2002
E-mail: Info@schifferbooks.com

For the largest selection of fine reference books on this and related subjects, please visit our website at
www.schifferbooks.com
We are always looking for people to write books on new and related subjects. If you have an idea for a book, please contact us at proposals@schifferbooks.com

This book may be purchased from the publisher.
Please try your bookstore first.
You may write for a free catalog.

In Europe, Schiffer books are distributed by
Bushwood Books
6 Marksbury Ave.
Kew Gardens
Surrey TW9 4JF England
Phone: 44 (0) 20 8392 8585; Fax: 44 (0) 20 8392 9876
E-mail: info@bushwoodbooks.co.uk
Website: www.bushwoodbooks.co.uk

DEDICATED

to the men

who with great enterprise

and inventiveness put power

behind saws and produced

the world's most useful

product

INTRODUCTION

The sawing of lumber has gone on continuously in the Pacific Northwest since 1825, when Governor George Simpson of the Hudson's Bay Company raised the British Union Jack above new Fort Vancouver. Some two years later he left this order for Dr. McLoughlin:

"The Sawmill will require 8 men and should be kept constantly at Work, as I expect fully as much advantage will be derived from the Timber as from the Coasting fur trade . . . I recommend that you build 2 vessels of 200 tons each for the Timber trade . . ."

The Northwest's pioneering missionaries, the Rev. Jason Lee, Dr. Marcus Whitman and the Rev. Henry Harmon Spalding, were all sawmill men and carpenters of some experience, as well as persons of professional education. Dr. Whitman, while practicing medicine, had been a partner in a Yates County, New York, sawmill. The first missionaries of the Northwest did "the very hard work of pit sawing" to produce their first construction lumber. Jason Lee built water-power sawmills at Salem in 1840 and at Willamette Falls in 1841. It was four years later before Dr. Marcus Whitman was sawing lumber to the creaking of a waterwheel. The site was 20 miles up the Walla Walla River from his mission, in the yellow pines of the Blue Mountains. At the time of the "Whitman Massacre," in November, 1847, 40,000 board feet of lumber were in stacks at Waiilatpu Mission, as material for the building of a school.

In 1847 the American trail-blazer on Puget Sound, Michael Simmons, erected a water-power sawmill at the site of today's Tumwater and a famous brewery. He sold the mill to Cranick Crosby and moved to Mason Couny in 1853, to build the first sawmill in that historic area.

Four steam sawmills were started on the shores of Puget Sound in 1853, beside ten that were powered by waterwheels. Pit sawing remained a common practice among the settlers, who also learned to split planks and shakes from straight-grained logs of Western red cedar.

In 1856 lumber trade with Japan was added to the ever-growing California market for the products of Northwest sawmills. Pope & Talbot, starting at Port Gamble in 1853, have sawed lumber right on through the years. In the 1880s they had 84 lumber carriers sailing in world trade.

Railroads were built, over the mountains from the Midwest and up from California valleys, to haul Western fir, cedar and pine lumber to rich farm-building markets. Montana, Idaho, Washington, Oregon and Northern California, began to grow into the giant lumber-producing region of today — the greatest sawmilling area in all the world.

Here is Ralph Andrews' story of that triumphant growth and its undying promise, shown in superb photography and told in true and vital words. The utilitarian waterwheel, the great days of the steam sawmill, the epic courage of the schooner masters, are glorified here. And this glory is rooted in reality on every page, each scene projected with basic facts. This a backward look at West Coast sawmilling — by the holy old mackinaw!

JAMES STEVENS

This Was Sawmilling ... Contents

WATER WHEELS IN THE WEST.. 11
    Georgetown Mill Had Long Career............................... 17
    Big Waterwheel Turned But Fidalgo City Died.......... 19
    The Old Deter Mill.. 20
    Waterpower On Tidewater... 23
    Steam Replaces Waterpower.. 26
    Sawmilling In Klamath 1900-1943.............................. 28
TIMBER VENTURES AND ADVENTURES............................ 31
    Pioneer Lumbering In Montana.................................. 32
    Echoes From The Spokane Pines................................ 39
    Sawmilling At Silverton... 42
    Drama In The Sugar Pine... 43
    When Sawmilling Was Two-Handled.......................... 44
GULLET CRACKS 45
    Thomas Askew's Dream Came True............................ 54
    McLaren Mill Grows Up.. 57
    Alberni's Famed Five... 58
    Historic Westport... 61
MILLS FOR THE RAIL TRADE... 63
    The Night Shift.. 64
    The White River Story... 69
    Gold Rush Started Olympic Area Lumbering.............. 73
    Sawmills Of Southwestern Siskiyou........................... 75
TIMBER AT TIDEWATER... 77
    Home Of The Brave And The Free............................. 86
    Fabulous And Famous.. 89
    Prayer In The Planing Mill.. 94
    "Spotless Town" Gone But Not Forgotten.................. 95
    Portland Harbor Sawmills.. 99
    Three Whistles Saved The Mill..................................102
    Brookings Had A Sawmill..105
    Lumber On The High Seas...107
    Coos Bay Goes Sawmilling..111
    Mendocino County Has Colorful Past........................115
    The Cook House Is Gone...126
    Marvellous One-Man Sawmill....................................128
CLEARS AND STARS..131
    The Influence Of Swedish Breakfast Food On The Lumber Industry......140
WATER LINES TO MILL AND MARKET.................................149
    Silvertip's Ride..149
SAWS AND MEN..157
    Sawmill Sign Language...159
    Sawyers And Setters...161
    Filers Are Key Men In The Mills...............................163
STIFFS AND SAVAGES...167
    Erickson's 169
    "Free Fare To Happy Valley"......................................174

WATER WHEELS
in the West

"Yes, I knew the Gordon mill. It was one of those up and down affairs — up today and down tomorrow. Grandpap used to start the saw in the log then go away, sometimes catch a fish, then after a while go back to see what effect the saw had had on the log."

This whimsical reference, credited to an old-timer of Bonanza, in Klamath County, Oregon, makes it easier to understand the facts and circumstances surrounding the first sawmills of the West Coast — the mills powered by little creeks and water wheels.

Frank Nichols, also of Bonanza, who operated one of these sash mills in the early '80s, said:

"It didn't cost much to make lumber in those days since I cut free government timber, then hired a man and team to haul in the logs. I ran the mill by myself so I didn't have any payroll to meet, and the only supply bill was for axle grease for the sash saw."

The sash mills were very crude in construction, most of the equipment homemade, largely of wood, and all powered with old-fashioned water wheels. In areas with sufficient head of water the "overshot" type of wheel was used. A low head of water demanded the "undershot" type.

Overshot wheels were built of wood with the diameter about the same as the waterhead, usually about eight feet, and with paddles or boxes four or five feet long. The undershot wheel used a log, eight to twelve inches in diameter for the shaft, with 2x4 or 2x6 paddles about ten feet long fastened on the log lengthwise — the wheel about two feet in diameter, ten feet long. The water flowed under the wheel, hence the name "undershot."

With either type an iron crank was fastened to the end of the shaft with a wooden connecting rod transmitting the up-and-down motion to the sash or wooden saw frame, about four feet wide and six to eight feet high. The "muley" was held taut by an overhead spring pole as crank operated it, steadied by wooden guides. The saw blade of very heavy gauge was from eight to twelve inches wide, six to eight feet long, secured to the extended rails of the sash. Sometimes two saws were used in this frame.

The carriage was pulled by a cable wrapped around a drum mounted on a shaft which was turned by a cast iron ratchet bolted on the side of a wooden wheel about four feet in diameter. With each revolution of the crank shaft, a dog engaged the ratchet and advanced the car-

(opposite) **CREEK POWER MADE LUMBER** Classic photograph of stream water in action making power for early Oregon sawmill. As late as 1904, 10% of U.S. sawmills used waterwheels. (U.S. Forest Service photo from W. C. Lumbermen's Association)

(below) **JAMES CLARKE MILL AT SPRUCE CREEK—ATLIN** Flume water turned power wheel in this early day mill. (Photo British Columbia Provincial Archives)

STUART LAKE WATERPOWER MILL in Fort George district, 1924. (Photo courtesy British Columbia Forest Service)

riage just enough for the next cut of the saw, thus constituting an automatic feed. Another device disengaged the dog when the saw line was finished, providing an automatic carriage stop. Water turned upon a small water wheel would gig the carriage back.

It required only one man to operate the entire mill. With the automatic carriage feed and stop he would simply start the carriage, then leave it while he took care of the lumber, slabs and edgings. When the saw line was finished he would return to the operation, gig back the carriage and set the log for the next cut with a pinch bar used first on one end of the log, then the other. When the log was squared, the side lumber was piled on top of it so that the next run of the carriage would edge it. Sash mills usually cut from 500 to 1500 feet a day, depending upon the water availability.

The better mills had circular head saws and were run by water turbines which developed much more power with the same amount and head of water. The circular saws were cutting all the time in the log, the sash saws less than half.

Most of the very early Western mills sawed logs from homesteads or helped themselves to government timber. Lumber was sold at the mill and $10 a thousand was considered standard for log run of grades.

There were water-powered mills in all the Coast states and British Columbia in those early days, including the shingle mills in the redwood areas of California and the cedar of Washington. It is estimated that as late as 1910, 10% of the lumber cut in the West was by water power.

The U.S. Government operated several of these saw-mills in its Indian agencies. In 1870 it built a circular mill powered by a water turbine at Klamath Agency, capacity probably three thousand feet a day. At completion of mill, Capt. O. C. Knapp, sub-agent, reported . . . "today cut from a log 18 feet long, 10 inches in diameter, 10 planks in four minutes." The following year, J. N. High, sub-agent, stated:

"The completion of the saw-mill has worked a great reformation and inspired them (the Indians) to extraordinary exertion to amass various kinds of property.

WATER POWER AT THE DALLES Manchester and Lester waterpower sawmill at Five Mile Creek, Oregon, about 1908. (Photo courtesy G. E. Manchester)

Savages in skins, paints, and feathers, as they were two short years since they have donned the white man's costume, taken the ax and cross-cut saw and hauled to the mill a half-million feet of lumber and today are lumber merchants with stock in trade constantly on hand evincing shrewdness and business integrity that make an agent's heart strong to work with and for them."

Indian Agent O. C. Applegate, in his annual report for 1900, stated:

"The only sawmill now in operation on this Reservation; the antiquated water mill located at this Agency and constructed 30 years ago, cannot begin to supply the lumber required for use by the Indians — age and long use have impaired its capabilities and 30 years of almost continuous operation have exhausted the available timber for many miles."

But private mills had sprung up all over the Coast. John Halsey Jones, founder of Portland's Jones Lumber Co. had first invested his savings in timber on Cedar Creek and with his father, Justus Jones, built an up-and-down sash mill with water wheel. Earlier than this the Hudson's Bay Co. mill at Fort Vancouver, a mill at Oregon City and Henry Hunt's mill on the Oregon side of the Columbia were cutting and shipping boards milled by water. About 1880 came another mill of the same type — Hunt and Martin's at Tongue Point. Miners on the Coquille River had a sash saw operation as did Julius

Hult at Colton in Clackamas County, E. P. Castleman in Lane County and the Myrtle Grove Mill built by Grube, Pohl and Rink in Coos County — all in Oregon. Washington had dozens of water-powered sawmills, starting with Michael Simmons' at Tumwater and the Willy mill at Allyn.

Details are given of the Naylor and Hockenhouse mill built on Spencer Creek in the Klamath Basin, Oregon, in 1869. It was a "muley" rig, the sawing unit being similar to a gang saw, and was propelled by water power. This mill could cut about 1,200 feet of lumber per day. The carriage had no head blocks, the log being set up on the carriage by means of a pinch bar while the power was turned off. This mill cut the lumber for the first bridge across the Link River at Linkville — now Klamath Falls. H. E. Spencer purchased this mill in 1870, operating until 1886.

There was the first Daniel "Grandpap" Gordon mill in Scott's Valley near Yreka, California, and the second on the south bank of the Klamath River about a mile west of Keno. It was a sash mill, powered by an overshot water wheel and had a capacity of 1500 feet a day. In 1875, Gordon sold the mill to his son-in-law, Newton W. Pratt, who in turn sold it to Charles Withrow a few years later, R. E. Dusenberry buying it in 1888.

Prior to 1880, the Cooper Brothers built a water turbine, circular mill on the north side of the Klamath

13

near Cooper Stage Station, about three miles west of Keno. This mill could cut three or four thousand feet of lumber but was handicapped by insufficient water due to a long, small canal. In '88, Herbert Cooper and Dusenberry took the better part of both mills to the better Dusenberry site, borrowing a large amount of money from Dan Van Bremer, on notes secured by mortgage, building 10,000 feet mill. The notes became delinquent. Van Bremer foreclosed and took the property. In 1892 Van Bremer then sold to Thomas McCormick, who ran the mill until 1909. The machinery was afterward moved to Sheep Mountain, fifteen miles south of Dorris, California.

In 1895 John Connolly built a sash mill on the Klamath River, at his ranch about a mile down river from the present highway crossing west of Keno. Since the water was insufficient, this mill sawed only 400 to 500 feet per day.

"Grandpap" Gordon built the first mill in the Bonanza district in 1876 or 1877. This was a sash mill, run by an undershot water wheel, and was located on the east bank of Lost River, one-eighth of a mile south of Bonanza, opposite the lower end of the island at that point. This mill ceased operation about 1883.

In 1880 or before, Orson Lewis built a similar mill for G. B. Van Riper on the west bank of the river, opposite the Gordon mill. The island provided each mill with a separate channel of the river, but that did not prevent trouble over the water question, since the volume was insufficient for both mills. Van Riper hauled logs about four miles with oxen and wagons and cut 700 or 800 feet per day. About 1882 he sold out to a nephew of Lewis, Frank Nichols who doubled the capacity of the mill by logging with horses and wagons, operating it until 1885.

Now let T. T. Gear tell of his personal experiences in the Grande Ronde Valley. (From "Fifty Years In Oregon," T. T. Gear, The Neale Publishing Co. N. Y. 1916.)

"The first summer I was in the Cove, 1867 (Union County, Grande Ronde Valley), my father hired me out to a Mr. McLoughlin who owned a sawmill on Mill Creek, two miles away. We had moved on a piece of land consisting of 40 acres, perfectly new, and had obtained the lumber for a very cheap house from Mr. McLoughlin, agreeing to pay for the greater part of it as we could. It was partly to discharge this obligation that I became his helper for a couple of months. It was the only sawmill within a distance of ten miles and the only one of its kind on the Pacific Coast — I should hope. It was driven by an overshot wheel, twenty-four feet in diameter and thirty inches wide, which required three minutes to make one revolution, and the machinery was so geared up that every time the wheel revolved once the

WATER AND MULE POWER ran the Hult Lumber Co. mill at Colton, Oregon, in 1906. Julius, Oscar and Phillip Hult named the mule Budweiser and worked ten hours a day to build a business. (Photo courtesy West Coast Lumbermen's Association)

OLD INDIAN SAWMILL — PRINCE RUPERT AREA. (Photo British Columbia Forest Service)

sash saw would be raised and lowered at least ten times. The cog gearing was made of fir blocks and would wear out after one week of service, making necessary the replacing of one every hour or two, while the only belt was the one reaching to the drum to which the sash was attached. This belt, made of cow skins, with the hair still on one side, would stretch to such an extent that when we were not making a new block for the cog we were taking up the slack. We made a new one one day which measured forty feet. The first afternoon we used it we cut out a surplus foot four times, and by the time it was worn out — it lasted a week — we had fifty feet of surplus hide and still forty feet of belt. There was no waste material about the mill anywhere.

"My special task in this work was to 'offbear' the mill's output, to do which, however, was not difficult. The logs were delivered on a hillside just above the mill by a team of oxen, and we could easily saw one every half-day. When we wanted a new log, we cleared the mill of all obstructions and removed the 'chunk' which retained the 'boom' on the hillside. This done, the log would surrender to the law of gravitation and with great velocity roll into the mill, usually taking its place on the

carriage without assistance. In fact, the speed made by the logs in this operation was the only rapid motion ever seen about the mill, and was an event to which we looked forward with great interest twice a day.

"But the one feature about that mill which I enjoyed to the full was the progress of the carriage as it pushed the log into the saw. It was a constant struggle as to which would surrender. Sometimes the saw would give up, and as the carriage endeavored to proceed against the dead saw, the mill would shake and tremble for a moment and all motion would cease, while the water would pour over the stationary wheel until the extra force would cause the belt to slip, when the wheel would turn halfway over, empty out its buckets and again come to a standstill. Sometimes a cog in the carriage gearing would break while the saw was savagely eating its way through a pine knot and, having no resistance, the remaining machinery would virtually run away with itself until the excited 'foreman' succeeded in shutting off the water. Oh, there were times when things were exciting in that old mill!

"But when everything was running smoothly it was great fun. Having 'set' the log and started the works

POWER FLUME RAN UP HILL? Camera angle distorts water line of Charles Brown's waterpower mill two miles south of Grangeville, Idaho. (Photo Idaho Historical Society)

going, there was a good long rest in store until the saw reached the further end. There was nothing unseemly about the gait of the carriage. It was deliberate part of the time. With the screws turned, the 'dogs' firmly driven in and the water turned on, as soon as the big wheel became filled, the picnic began. Mr. McLoughlin was a devoted reader of the Weekly Oregonian, and after he had satisfied himself that the belt was not going to slip on that trip, he would settle himself on the log and begin reading one of Mr. Scott's editorials, for which he had great admiration. Sitting on a gunnysack filled with straw, which he used as a cushion, his happiest moments I am sure were those which found him deeply buried in the columns of the Oregonian, the music of the saw mingling with the splash of the pouring water, indicating to his subconscious mind that all was well, that the gait he was traveling was not transcending the speed limit, and that sometime before dinner there would be another contribution to the world's lumber supply.

"Of course, in a mill of this character it was utter impossible to saw lumber accurately. Nearly all planks intended to be an inch thick were two inches at one end and half an inch at the other — often a mere feather in the middle. For this reason the house we built was a foot wider at one end and narrower in the middle than at either end and we had great difficulty in making a roof that would force water to run from its comb to the eaves.

"One day a cottonwood log was brought in from the woods and Mr. McLoughlin concluded that, as it was soft material, it would be a good thing to saw it up into thin stuff, half-inch thick, to be used probably for making boxes of some sort. This was done or rather attempted. On account of the uncertain cut of the saw it usually used up an inch of material as it went hammering its way through a log, and to get a half-inch board from this process was not only a fearful waste of raw material but the precise result obtained was a matter of the wildest conjecture. However, we sawed up that cottonwood log, three feet in diameter, got seven thin boards — and a wagon load of sawdust. I stacked them out in the sun in a loose pile to season, and within three days they had warped themselves out of the lumberyard and were found in a neighbor's corral a mile down the creek.

"In 1870 Mr. McLoughlin sold his mill and moved to the Willamette Valley, settling on the Abiqua, near Silverton, where he died soon afterwards. Two years ago (in 1910, presumably) when on a visit to the Cove, I sauntered across to the old mill site but there was no sign anywhere that there had been a mill there — that the hum and buzz of a great manufacturing establishment ever disturbed the local quiet by its sporadic efforts to supply the local market with lumber. All was changed and there was in place of the old mill a pretty garden in front of a cozy cottage, with two children playing where the logs used to rumble down the hillside."

OLDEST SAWMILL IN NORTHERN B.C. Famous Georgetown mill built of hewn timber by George Williscroft in 1875 on Big Bay, 17 miles north of Prince Rupert. Water wheel was used for power at first giving an output of 5000 feet a day. Mill was improved and after George Williscroft's death in 1895, operated by his brother W. A. Williscroft and several other succeeding companies including Big Bay Lumber Company. (Photo British Columbia Forest Service)

GEORGETOWN MILL HAD A LONG CAREER

At Georgetown, seventeen miles north of Prince Rupert, the Big Bay Lumber Co. operated the oldest sawmill in Northern British Columbia, one which had its beginning in the water-power era. The company, in the persons of H. R. MacMillan and George McAfee of Georgetown, leased the mill in 1918 and the following year bought both plant and wharf.

The Georgetown mill was established in 1875 by George Williscroft. C. F. Morrison, of Metkakatla, was interested with him in the original establishment of the mill.

The old original mill of 1875, which was a unique part of the plant as late as 1920, was built of hewn timber. A water wheel was used for power and the output was about 5,000 feet per day. Williscroft kept enlarging and improving the plant right along until its output was raised to 20,000 feet. Among the improvements was the putting in of a water turbine to supplement the power.

The mill supplied the most of the local trade of the early days and box lumber was manufactured for the canneries of the Skeena, Naas, Rivers Inlet and Alert Bay. One of the first shipments ever sent to the Yukon country was made by the Georgetown mill.

The old steamer Nell was built here by the original company and was used for the towing of logs and the distribution of the finished product. It was a twin screw vessel and made monthly trips to Victoria. Captain William Madden and Captain William Oliver were well known at various times as the masters of the boat.

George Williscroft owned and operated the mill until his death in 1895, after which W. A. Williscroft, his brother, operated it for three years for the trustees. After this a new company, of which James Brown, now of Port Essington, Capt. William Oliver, and a number of missionaries, were members, took it over and operated it until 1907 when Haliburton Peck and brothers and Dr. W. T. Kergin bought it. They carried on for eleven years steadily adding improvements and increasing the output. Walter H. Williscroft, son of George Williscroft, was in charge of the mill for the Peck and Kergin interests for many years and R. H. Cole, who later went to Sandspit, was storekeeper and accountant. It was during the control of these interests that the steamer *Nell*, which was used right along in connection with the mill, was caught in a south easter off Metlakatla and, going ashore in Duncan's Cove, went to pieces.

(opposite) **MILL IN MIGHT-HAVE-BEEN CITY**
Ed Knapp's waterpowered sawmill on Deception
Pass on Puget Sound, site of highly promoted
Fidalgo City which never got a start. Flume car-
ried water off hill to the 35 foot wheel. (Photo
Stacey Collection, Mt. Vernon)

WOODEN BUT THEY WORKED Gears fashioned
from hardwood by which power from revolving
water wheel was transmitted to saws in waterpower mills. Gear cogs were individually cut and
inserted in solid wood wheels. (U.S. Forest Service
photo from W. C. Lumbermen's Association)

BIG WATERWHEEL TURNED . . . BUT
FIDALGO CITY DIED

In 1890 it looked to people around Puget Sound that
the hamlet of Dewey, on Deception Pass, had a sparkling
future. It had a water-powered sawmill with a 35-foot
wheel owned by Ed Knapp. It had a 40-room hotel operated by a Mr. Van Loon. It had general stores run by
W. H. Halpin and C. J. Carlyle. It even had a 3-story
bank building built by Will Potter and his brother Julius.

But the best reason for Fidalgo City's bright future
was that F. J. Carlyle and George Loucke had made a
plat of the metropolis-to-be on Fidalgo Island. 341 blocks
were surveyed and the first day lots went on sale. 252
of them were snapped up, not only by local people but
by buyers in New England. Even an electric interurban
line was expected to run from bustling Anacortes, the
rails already laid.

This was the situation the day the Rothschild bank
in England failed, the spark that set off the financial
panic in 1893. Disastrous all over the world, it swept
Fidalgo City right into Puget Sound as it were, a blow
from which it never recovered. The city-in-prospect went
back to just Dewey and the people who paid $3000 for
lots later sold them for $20 and were glad to get it.
The bank building became a housing project for 2600
chickens.

Ed Knapp went on sawing timber in his waterpower
mill. Most of the men around Dewey worked here or
logged into the Sound and towed the fir to the mill by
rowboat. Others cut wood for the boilers of the steamers
or towed the cut lumber to market in Port Angeles. But
the timber receded and the log haul got too expensive.
The mill was never rebuilt and its ghost joined that of the
saloons and hotel of the city-that-never-was.

19

AND LOG WAS FED BY HAND Early sash or up-and-down saw powered by waterwheel. At first, short log was inched into saw by hand, later ratcheted by waterpower. (U.S. Forest Service photo from W. C. Lumbermen's Association)

THE OLD DETER MILL

by LILLIAN DETER BALIS
In Siskiyou County Historical Society Yearbook 1948

The Deter Mill, at the foot of Goosenest, was built by my father, George W. Deter, in 1881 and operated by him for 14 years. This sawmill supplied lumber to Butte Valley, Shasta Valley, the Klamath River and for many of the fine homes in Yreka. The old ferry boat at Anderson's Ferry was built of lumber and timbers from this mill.

Shortly after my father and mother were married in Yreka in 1868, they bought a farm in Little Shasta from a Frenchman named Poncho. (This farm is known as the old Janson place and now owned by Dale Burke.) Three of us children were born on this farm and our family lived here until we were obliged to move to a higher altitude because of my mother's health. Father sold the farm and went to the foot of Goosenest where he took a homestead on the site where he later built a sawmill. Nestled at the foot of Goosenest Mountain on Little Shasta Creek, on the main road over Ball Mountain, this beautiful spot was named "Forest Vale" by my

father. Being the only stopping place between the Ball Ranch and Shasta Valley, our house soon became an overnight stop for travelers. Later, father built a large 20-room hotel which became very well known as the Deter Hotel.

Father went to work at the old Cleland Sawmill four miles below our place. He would walk the four miles, work in the mill from six in the morning until six at night, and walk back home again. After two or three years this mill shut down and father began selling shakes and shingles which he made by hand. Having a few cows he also made cheese to sell.

As there were no sawmills in operation any place near, the Shasta Valley farmers persuaded father to build a mill on his home place. So in the spring of 1881, he hired two men to go with him into the fine timber which surrounded our home and hew out the lumber for the frame and all needed to build trestles etc. for the mill. Next he made the shingles to cover it. All the work was

done by hand. Nails were so scarce he sat up nights to make wooden pins out of old wagon spokes. The timbers had to be mortised out and holes bored in the end to drive the pins through and hold the corners together.

After putting up the frame, roofing it all and laying the flooring, father sawed out all the lumber to finish the mill satisfactorily. Pulleys and wheels had to be made of wood, as there was no railroad this side of Redding over which to ship iron pulleys etc. There were long tramways and high trestles to build and a mile of ditch to dig. This ditch or mill race was 5 feet wide and 3 to 4 feet deep.

Water to furnish power for the mill was taken from Little Shasta Creek and a flume about 300 feet long carried the water from the mill race to a penstock through which it dropped onto a turbine wheel at the bottom. This penstock or pipe, built by the side of the mill was 40 feet high and 5 feet square and was made of 4 inch by 8 inch plank mortised in. The mill was built in a gulch-like spot, a drop of about 25 or 30 feet below ground level. So that brought the saw, carriages and logs on the first floor. All the big belts and main machinery were placed under the floor.

One of the most tedious tasks was the building of the coal pit to supply coals for the blacksmith shop. A small pile of kindling was placed on a level spot and

small short limbs put around it in a circle. Gradually longer limbs were used, leaning them to the center and leaving a small hole on one side to start the fire. After the small limbs were on, larger ones of yellow pine 4 or 5 inches across, were used. The pit could be any desired size but this one was about 12 feet across and 8 feet high. It was built like an Indian wigwam — large at the bottom and small at the top (about 5 feet). The limbs were placed close together all around until the pit would measure 12 feet across the bottom, then hay or straw was placed all over it and half stove pipes placed around about every 8 feet, halfway up, for ventilation. Then dirt was spread all over it — 5 inches deep to keep out all air. Now it was lit and let burn to get well started. Then the holes were plugged to put out the fire and leave the coals to smoulder for a short time. One or two pipes would then be opened to let in air enough to keep it from dying out. It would have to be watched day and night for eight or ten days to keep it from getting on fire; if it did all holes would be plugged up for a time. The pit wouldn't be opened for several days or until it was all cold. Then the coal was spread over the ground and we children carried water over any live coals we saw.

The building of the two big ox trucks was another big undertaking. From the woods a clear yellow pine tree about 4 feet through was cut down and eight cuts of 4 feet each were sawed off for the wheels. These were hauled to the blacksmith shop, the bark removed and a tire about 8 inches wide placed on each wheel (the tires had been bought from another mill). One side was to be inside next to the truck bed, the other trimmed out on a bevel to about 24 inches all around the wheel and a hole made in the center about 8 inches wide to insert an iron spindle to fit on the axle. It was a big job to "iron the trucks all off," as it was called, and make them strong enough to hold up the big logs we had in those days.

At off times during the building of the mill father worked on smaller jobs, such as making grease. Beef tallow did not wear long enough for greasing ox trucks, so he made his own grease by getting a pitch stump, cutting it up fine and filling a big old iron kettle full of it. The kettle would then be turned upside down on a big piece of sheet iron which had a bent place in it so the pitch could run out. The pitch was set on fire and let burn under the kettle which was lifted a bit until it got to burning. As the pitch started to run out, the kettle was let down, putting the fire out enough so it just smouldered for hours until all the pitch had run out into a big bucket. Then beef tallow was mixed in with it until it was the consistency of axle grease. This was used for all greasing about the mill as well as on the ox trucks.

Other tasks, such as tanning small beef hides for small pulleys, and making deer hides into lacing, kept father busy far into the night. Finally the mill was ready for the machinery. Father hired a millwright to place the machinery in order but he got it in wrong and it wouldn't work. Oh, the hard time my father had to get it in running order for there were very few men who knew how to place machinery in a sawmill.

In May of 1882, father went out to the valley as it was then called (now Weed or Mt. Shasta) to buy oxen for his log hauling. He bought some of Mr. Dave Elton and some from the old Maxwell Mill (the Dobkins people). When he got home with his 16 head of oxen and 8 yokes, he built a platform and chute for shoeing them. He had to make all the iron shoes but had a fine blacksmith to do the work.

In late May the mill was ready for operation. After a year an edger was installed. Then in another year and a half father put in a planer. But the stream of water did not furnish power enough to run both saws and planer so he had to run the saws in the daytime and planer at night. He was head sawyer and then would run the planer from 7 p.m. until 2 and 3 a.m. I could never see how he stood the hard, long hours! This mill was large enough to cut 30 thousand feet a day which it did early in the spring. But the water did not hold out long and the average was from 20 to 25 thousand and even less as the fall came. In those days it was possible to saw more lumber per day than one might expect, due to longer working hours, the heavy timber close at hand and the demand for so many large timbers such as used in barns and granaries.

After operating the mill for about fourteen years, father sold it to Mr. Hugo Miller. To the best of my knowledge Mr. Miller operated it for two or three years, then sold the machinery and shut down the mill. Some years later the property came into the hands of Harcourt G. Biggs and Reginald Mills. Mr. and Mrs. Mills, an English couple, spent a number of happy years there, cultivating a small garden, raising chickens and hogs and milking a few cows. From these people, this pretty little mountain valley comes by the name it is now known as — "The Mills Ranch," and Forest Vale has passed on to history. On Nov. 6, 1916, the property was sold from Mills and Biggs to Charles Soule, though Reginald Mills and his wife reserved the right to live there which they did for a few more years. At the present time the land is owned by John Soule of Edgewood who uses it as a summer pasture for his cattle.

Above all the hardships we endured at Forest Vale, it was the happiest time of our lives. The last three children of our family were born there and mother, though an invalid, made all our clothes by hand including the tatting, crocheting etc. for trimming.

INDIANS CUT 2000 FEET A DAY in this old sawmill at Aiyansh in 1913. (Photo British Columbia Provincial Archives)

WATERPOWER ON TIDEWATER

The brig *Chenamus* was leaving the dock headed down the Columbia River for the open sea. She carried the first cargo from Oregon's first independent, American-owned, export mill—fifty thousand feet of two by fours and one-inch boards sawed in a mill with three thousand feet capacity in a twelve-hour day.

The sawmill was the pride and joy of Henry H. Hunt who had hauled the "mill irons" from Ohio across the plains by oxen and prairie schooner. The mill irons consisted of the headrig, iron crankshaft, an assortment of iron bolts and a set of millwright's tools.

Henry Hunt was 33, fit and bull strong when he arrived at Oregon City in 1843. He was also intelligent and saw at once the sawmills at Willamette Falls and the Hudson's Bay mill at Fort Vancouver were not well located for export trade. Sailing vessels had too hard a time getting up the Columbia under canvas. Why not locate a mill near the mouth of the Columbia at a place where there was plenty of creek water?

There was no way of getting down river except in it since both banks were covered with trackless virgin forests of big firs and cedars. So Henry Hunt sold his ox team and bought a flatboat, at the same time picking

up a partner—Tallmadge Benjamin Wood, a 26 year old New Yorker. The pair then took in as a third man, Edwin M. Otey, a millwright. The three loaded the boat with the mill irons, provisions, blankets, cooking utensils and personal gear and took off down the Willamette.

Ben Wood and Otey steered with paddles past the future site of Portland, keeping their eyes open for likely spots to build a sawmill. Hunt was not interested until they paddled past the area of the present St. Helens and on down until they came to a stream about two and a half miles beyond what would be Clifton. He was afraid to go further as he did not know just where the mouth of the Columbia was or that there was no activity between them and the mouth, only a Scotsman's shanty at Astoria.

The three partners tied up and unloaded their craft. They built a cabin and began work on the mill. They hewed timbers, split planks and shakes, constructed a twenty foot water wheel at the bottom of the canyon where the creek gave them a sixty foot fall. They rigged up a whip saw and cut boards for the mill, connected the crankshaft to the wheel, put the mill saw in a frame and the frame between uprights so it could slide up and

MILL AT MOODYVILLE ON BURRARD INLET—1885. (Photo British Columbia Provincial Archives)

down. Gears and cog wheels were shaped and whittled from oak or crabapple wood. They rolled the bucked logs directly into the mill from the hillsides and planned on floating the sawn lumber downstream to the cargo ships which would be putting in. But it was a year before the mill cut its first log.

Meanwhile news of Hunt's new mill was going around Oregon City and hungry men showed up for work. Hunt started the mill with fifteen of them, paying what cash he could with orders on merchants Allen and McKinley and Pettygrove and Abernethy — both in Oregon City — and on Hudson's Bay in Fort Vancouver. This paper became known as "scrip and grindstones." For when a merchant doubted the worth of the paper, he said he was out of everything but some old grindstones.

Hunt's mill turned out boards, planks and scantlings, twelve to fourteen feet long. Logs were rolled on the mill deck with a crowbar, fed to the saw by a ratchet arrangement called a "ragwheel," then for the next cut pried over again with the crowbar. As the water wheel turned so turned the master wheel on the same shaft. This meshed into the counter wheel which meshed into a wheel on the crankshaft. As the wheels revolved, the saw

moved up and down, cutting on the downstroke only. Scantlings were cut in blocks, with several saws in the sash or frame, a process forerunning the gang saw. The cut was stopped short of the end so some solid timber could hold boards together until carpenters were ready to use them.

When water was abundant in the creek, Hunt's mill sawed 10 thousand feet in twenty-four hours but this was not every day. The men were lucky to have 50 thousand feet when the brig *Chenamus* hove to and took the whole stock. Other ships made Hunt's mill a regular stop, among them the bark *Toulon* and brig *Henry*.

When the three partner's had been operating a year, Astoria had grown to a settlement of 30 white people. Storekeeper A. E. Wilson, Astoria's first white citizen bought Ben Wood's interest in the sawmill. He also brought in oxen for logging and five Kanakas, hired from King Kamehameha of the Sandwich Islands, paying them $5 a month, salmon and potatoes. In 1847 he sold out to Henry Hunt. Ben Wood had gone to California and been killed by sluice robbers at Spanish Bar.

Meanwhile another man bought into the Hunt enterprise — James Birnie, retired Hudson's Bay Co. factor

FIRST SAWMILL ON VANCOUVER ISLAND at Sooke. In 1853 John Meier acquired Capt. Grant's old waterpower mill where West Sooke is now, rebuilt and established lumber yard in Victoria. (Photo B.C. Provincial Archives)

who had founded Cathlamet on his land claim. His Hudson's Bay connections enabled the mill to get better provisions than it was getting from Oregon City or from Pettygrove's new store in the settlement of Portland.

In the summer of 1848 the brig *Henry* brought news of the California gold strike and Hunt's mill began to hum. He then bought the small mill of H. B. Polley, built at the mouth of the Clatskanie River. Then Hunt and Martin bought a third mill just above Tongue Point, beginning to saw here in 1949. Lumber prices were now soaring. 100 thousand feet at the original Hunt mill brought $100 a thousand.

But where to get sawmill workers? Almost every able bodied man had left for the California gold diggings. Clement Adams Bradbury, later a noted citizen, had been working for Henry Hunt, but with three other men built a twenty-ton boat, the *Wave*, took aboard a dozen passengers and headed down the Coast, arriving at San Francisco after 15 days. Hunt and Martin advertised their frantic need for men, especially sawyers, in the Oregon Spectator.

During 1949 the brig *Henry* and bark *Quito* took on regular cargoes at Hunt's mill at fabulous prices. Then the old packet, *Sylvia de Grasse*, built in New York of live oak and locust, the same vessel which had brought the first news of the French Revolution to the United States, anchored at Hunt's dock. Lured to the Pacific

by the gold rush, she had been bought by a man named Gray who had hastened north leaving orders for the *Sylvia* to follow.

Now she finished loading at Hunt's and with 600 thousand feet of lumber left for Astoria to pick up a pilot named Pickernell. However, when the anchor was raised, the packet drifted onto a submerged rock and went aground. Gray, frantic over the delay, tried in vain to find another ship. He offered the skipper of the newly arrived *Walpole* a $10,000 bonus to take on his lumber but being under U.S. charter, the skipper had to refuse. Weeks passed and Gray fumed. Finally he secured three small schooners and divided his lumber among them but by that time prices had fallen and his chance at a fortune was lost. The *Sylvia de Grasse* sank but her timbers were still good enough in 1894 for an Astoria ship builder to cut a section out of her hull for another ship.

With lumber prices down, Hunt's sawmill went into a decline. Steam mills were beginning to come in and water power was too slow and expensive. But Henry Hunt went on. With S. Coffin he built a ship in New York City to ply between Oregon City and San Francisco and became a longtime citizen of Clatsop County. By 1852 there were three steam sawmills and two water-power mills in the area.

PERKINS MILL—CARLTON cutting ties and rough lumber. Office and boarding house at left.
(Photo Oregon Collection, University of Oregon)

STEAM REPLACES WATER POWER

By 1885 it was fully evident that a West Coast lumber industry was growing well beyond the producing power of water wheels and sash saws. Stationary engines and boilers were being shipped west from Chicago and north from San Francisco. Circular saw equipment was being refined and with steam, mills could produce ten and twenty times the footage they had a few years earlier.

Steam and the circular saw arrived about the same time and sent the manufacture of lumber into a headlong pace. Then another element entered the picture — labor troubles. At an earlier time whip sawyers had opposed the introduction of water power fearing the loss of their jobs. Now the water power sawmill laborers looked with jaudiced eye on the new-fangled saw and boiler-driven machinery. Would it deprive them of their livelihood?

A hundred mills went through transformation and another hundred mill owners simply abandoned water power plants and built steam mills. The early history of lumbering in the Klamath area, given in a Lamm Lumber Co. publication, shows the rapid growth of early steam powered sawmills.

James P. Colahan built a circular mill on Bly Mountain, north of Bonanza, about 1885. Run by a steam traction engine, it was the first steam driven mill in the county and had a capacity of 5 thousand feet or more a day. This mill was portable and was often moved to various sites on Bly Mountain, probably to shorten the log haul. One site was the White Ranch in 1889, another Keno Springs in 1898.

Al Fitch built a steam driven circular mill near Hildebrand in 1894, the first mill in the area to have a stationary boiler and the fastest mill in Southern Oregon at that time, capable of cutting 15 to 20 thousand feet a day. The mill ceased operating in 1903 when Fitch was crushed by a log.

In 1888, Jesse D. Carr, owner of the Dalton Ranch, financed the building of a sawmill on Bryant Mountain, about ten miles northeast of Malin. This circular with stationary boiler and engine was operated by Rogers and McCoy until 1892.

William S. Moore, the most prominent pioneer lumberman of the county, had migrated from the Illinois plains to the Willamette Valley, moving to the Klamath Agency in 1868. Two years later he built the sawmill

MILL YARD OF SINCLAIR AND SCHULTZ Atlin, B.C. (Photo courtesy British Columbia Forest Service)

there for the government. In 1877, Moore built a sawmill on the west side of Link River, about half way between Linkville and Upper Klamath Lake. A canal was built from the lake to the mill to provide water for the turbine and also to float the logs to the mill. This was the finest site in the county since ample water power and an unlimited supply of timber were available. The mill equipment consisted of a water turbine, circular head saw, friction-driven carriage and a push feed ripsaw to edge the lumber. The capacity of the mill was eight to ten thousand feet per day with a crew of ten to twelve men.

In 1887 William Moore sold the mill to his two sons, Charles S. and Rufus S. Moore, after which it was known as the Moore Brothers' Mill. Later a planer was installed on the ground floor of the mill building in order to furnish surfaced lumber, flooring, and siding to the customers. This was the first planer installed in conjunction with a sawmill in the county. Lumber was sold right from the pile and loaded on the wagons of the customers,

as was the general custom in those days. This mill, the fourth private sawmill built in the county, had by far the steadiest and longest run of any of the early mills. The operation was unusually successful and continued until 1907, covering a period of thirty years.

At first logs were skidded into Shoal Water Bay with ox teams, and the rafts of logs were towed down the lake with a mule tread mill and a sail. Later horses and wagons supplanted the ox teams, the towing being done with a steam boat.

In 1891 John F. Goeller arrived in Linkville and purchased one-half interest in the planing mill and cabinet shop of A. M. Peterman. The name of the town was being changed to Klamath Falls and the firm name became The Klamath Falls Planing Mills. After a succession of partners, Goeller's son Harry entered the company, the business continued as J. F. Goeller and Son until 1920. It was sold that year and the plant burned a year or two later.

ALGOMA LUMBER COMPANY had bought the D. B. Campbell mill on Rattlesnake Point, Upper Klamath Lake, rebuilt and installed the machinery from Pokegama. E. J. Grant was part owner with Faye Fruit Co. and took over management in 1915. Plant was dismantled in 1943. (Photo courtesy H. H. Ogle)

KLAMATH FALLS IN 1913 At this time some of the sawmills operating in and near the city were Pelican Bay Lumber Co., Klamath Manufacturing Co., Ewauna Box Co., Algoma Lumber Co., Ackley Brothers, Long Lake Lumber Co., Big Basin Lumber Co. (Photo courtesy H. H. Ogle)

SAWMILLING IN KLAMATH 1900 - 1943

Shortly after the turn of the century, when it was learned that the Southern Pacific Railroad would build into Klamath Falls, lumbering in the county took heart, the smaller mills expanding and many new ones built. (From historical records given in Lamm Lumber Company presentation.)

Ray Potter built a small sawmill at Pokegama in 1903 which ceased operations in 1906. Four years later the Algoma Lumber Company built there and ran three seasons. High up on the northeast slope of Stukel Mountain in 1901, W. P. Rhoades built a circular mill, later the capacity almost doubled by adding another boiler and engine even though water had to be hauled from a spring a mile away. After operating four years this mill was sold to Turner Brothers who first moved it to the spring and then to a site two miles south of Olene.

In 1904 John and Harry Ackley purchased the Al Fitch sawmill near Hildebrand and moved it to Klamath Falls on Lake Ewauna. It was later leased and operated by Modoc Pine Company. About 1905 William Huson and Roscoe Cantrell built a circular mill of 20 M capacity on Long Lake operating under the name Long Lake Lumber Company. In 1908 the mill was moved to Shippington, the first sawmill on Upper Klamath Lake. It was sold and dismantled in 1915.

In 1907, after closing down their old sawmill on Link River, Moore Brothers built a fast, steam driven circular mill on the west shore of Klamath Lake, selling this plant in 1910 to Walter Innes and W. I. Clarke who operated as the Innes-Clarke Lumber Company for two years, and then sold in 1912 to the Big Basin Lumber Company, at that time a subsidiary concern of the Klamath Development Company. The plant was operated for an additional two seasons and closed in 1914.

The California Fruit Canner's Association in 1908 built the first box factory in the county, adjacent to the mill of the Long Lake Lumber Company at Shippington, and hired Charles McGowan as manager. This company shipped the first box shook from the county by hauling

KESTERSON MILL ON KLAMATH RIVER when completed in 1930. Kesterson Lumber Co. had been operating in Dorris, Calif., but reorganized and built mill two miles south of Klamath Falls using Long-Bell logs transported over Lamm Lumber Co. railroad and Southern Pacific. Later used timber from Walker and Henry's holdings. (Photo courtesy H. H. Ogle)

it in wagons to Pokegama, where it was shipped over the Klamath Lake Railroad to the California market. The factory was sold in 1912.

The railroad being completed into Klamath Falls in 1909, H. D. Mortenson came to Klamath in 1910 and organized the Pelican Bay Lumber Company, which contracted for a large unit of Government timber lying west of Pelican Bay in the Crater National Forest. The company, in 1911 built a complete and strictly modern sawmill plant with the first band head saw, the first shotgun carriage feed, and the first complete planing mill in the county, all entirely planned for supplying the United States markets. The plant had a capacity of about 60,000 feet per shift and was the first plant to run two shifts. Dry kilns were added in 1912. The sawmill burned in 1914 and was promptly rebuilt with a larger mill, consisting of two band head-rigs and a band resaw. In 1918 a fire destroyed this second mill, and it in turn was replaced with one of similar size. This third mill was the first completely electrified mill in the county and until 1926 was the largest mill. In 1921 a large box factory was added.

In 1914 W. E. Lamm organized the Lamm Lumber Company, and contracted for the Odessa unit of timber on the Crater National Forest. Logging operations started in January, 1915, and the logs produced that year were sawed at the Long Lake Lumber Company mill at Shippington under least. Late that year construction was started on a single band mill at Lelu (later Modoc Point) and operation started in the spring of 1916. Dry kilns, planing mill were added and in 1929 a resaw, in 1932 a box factory. The plant closed down in 1942 and was dismantled.

In 1916 Wilbur Knapp built a small circular mill on Williamson River, north of Chiloquin, selling out two years later to Modoc Lumber Company, operated by J. O. Goldthwaite, which concern sold out to the Forest Lumber Company in 1924, a larger, more modern mill being built. Fire destroyed the entire plant in 1939.

The Big Lake Box Company was organized in 1917 by A. J. Voye, M. S. West and Burge Mason and purchased the lumber yard property of Savidge Brothers in Klamath

FREE CIGARS WHEN CUT WAS 40 THOUSAND Collier mill at Swan Lake near Klamath Falls, Ore., in 1921. "This was some mill," says A. D. Collier. "Logs came in mill on rollway and tram cars. We usually got about 35 thousand feet in 9 hours with 50″ top and 44″ bottom saw, 2-block carriage with screw feed and hand setworks. When we hit 40 thousand all hands got free cigars. We had water buckets on the roof and open fires in the slab pit. This was sawmilling!" (Photo Collier Collection Collier State Park Logging Museum)

Falls, changing it into a box factory. In 1920 the company built a band mill on Lake Ewauna.

In 1917 Curt F. Setzer organized the Chelsea Box Company, which built a factory about a mile south of Klamath Falls. In 1920 the plant was sold to the Growers Packers and Warehousing Association. The factory burned in 1924, and the balance of the property was then sold to the Shaw Bertram Lumber Company.

In 1918 E. A. Blocklinger organized the Chiloquin Lumber Company which built a circular mill on the Sprague River at Chiloquin, and also put in a box factory. Later the mill was changed over to a single band plant.

In 1919 John Bedford and Harold Crane organized the Sprague River Lumber Company, which built a small circular mill on Sprague River, three miles east of Chiloquin. After operating two years, Mr. Bedford sold out in 1921 to William Bray, who later organized the Braymill White Pine Company, in which Mr. Crane retained an interest and became the manager. Part of the logs for this mill were shipped in from Mr. Bray's timber holdings in California and part were obtained from the Little Sprague unit of timber. The mill closed down in 1928.

J. R. Shaw and W. J. Bertram organized the Shaw-Bertram Lumber Company in 1920 with plant on Lake Ewauna which was sold to the Southern Pacific Company in 1934, subsequently leased to the Long-Bell Lumber Company who purchased it in 1939. Plant and timberlands were sold to Weyerhaeuser Timber Company in 1942.

Wheeler Olmstead Lumber Company built a mill north of Shippington in 1920 which operated intermittently. George McCullom built a mill on the Klamath

River west of Keno in 1920 which was sold to Ellingson Lumber Company in 1934. In 1924 the Shasta View Lumber Company, organized by Marion and Wilbur Nine built a small band mill in Klamath Falls, operating it a few years and in 1928 selling to Klamath Pine Lumber Company. Plant burned on July 4, 1929, and was not rebuilt.

In 1925 the Campbell Towle Lumber Company took over a small circular mill located at Sprague River and owned by Edgerton and Adams. In 1928 the company sold to G. C. Lorenz, who rebuilt the mill completely and operated it under the name of Lorenz Lumber Company, cutting timber from Cherry Creek, Rock Creek, and Whiskey Creek units. In the middle of 1930 the plant was sold to the Crater Lake Lumber Company, for whom Huntington Taylor was manager. In 1932 a box factory was added, and in 1937 the Crater Lake Box and Lumber Company was organized and operated the plant under lease from Crater Lake Lumber Company until December 28, 1942. Logs were obtained from Whiskey Creek, Bly-Brown Creek, Trout Creek, and Squaw Flat units of the Reservation and also from private holding. On January 1, 1943, the Crater Lake Lumber Company again started operations and continued until the fall of 1943 when the sawmill was shut down and dismantled; the box factory was then sold to the American Box Corporation, which is still operating it. Crater Lake Lumber Company has been selling logs since the middle of 1943 up to and including the present time, part of its logging operations being carried on under contract by the Beatty Logging Company.

TIMBER VENTURES
and Adventures

The Pioneer Sawmill

Overgrown with fern and brambles yonder in the clearing,
Ghostly in the moonlight lies an old, deserted mill,
Relic of departed days, the days of pioneering,
Strong days and clean days of steadfast faith and will.
Faint and clear
I seem to hear
The old saws' phantom singing,
Music merging with the steps of many marching men;
Eager feet and fearless, a larger freedom bringing,
The spirit of the fathers winging westward once again.

Meager days, if money be the measure of succeeding,
Golden days, if happiness from toil and simple ways;
Hewing out a new home, grim hardship's toil unheeding,
Living for the morrows by the light of yesterdays.
Well you fought,

Planned and wrought,
Taught by creeds rejected;
Enduring are the monuments in memory of your name—
Countless homes and happy, your deathless souls reflected
In hearth fires burning with freedom's sacred flame.

Silver sheen of moonlight clothes the ruin with new beauty,
Solemnly, in homage to an ever-glowing past.
The wind sighs. A star falls. The stillness speaks of duty,
The forest dreams of multitudes to build a future vast.
Sweet and clear
I can hear
Unborn voices singing
Strong in unison a song of fruitful days to come;
Voices full of gladness, a greater glory bringing
To your land, to my land, the land we love—our home.
. . . Charles Oluf Olsen

ANTON HOLTER'S SAWMILL on Stickney Creek, Montana, in 1880. See following story. (Photo from Norman Holter courtesy Historical Society of Montana)

PIONEER LUMBERING IN MONTANA

by ANTON M. HOLTER

These reminiscences appeared in The Timberman in 1911 and in The Frontier, University of Montana, in May, 1928. Anton Holter, born in Norway, was a carpenter in Decorah, Iowa. With $3000 in savings he and his brother set out for Colorado, settling in what is now Idaho Springs.

After three years' residence at Pikes Peak, I returned to my former home in Iowa and in the spring of 1863 started with a team of oxen back to Colorado, where I stopped about six weeks. During this time a company of 200 men was organized to go to what was then called Stinking Water, Idaho, but is now known as Ruby River, in Madison County, Montana.

This company left Colorado on September 16, 1863. It was well organized, having a captain and other officers, and was governed by a formal set of rules and regulations. The weather was pleasant and food for the stock was excellent. Hunting and fishing were especially fine — too much so in fact for so much time was spent in sport that we made slow progress, and finally a Mr. Evenson, and myself, became fearful that we would be unable to reach our destination before winter, and de-cided it was best for us to leave the train and strike out for ourselves at a greater rate of speed.

We had purchased a second-hand sawmill outfit, intending to go into the lumbering business on reaching our destination. There was yet at least a thousand miles to cover, so one morning we yoked up our oxen and struck out alone. During the night a few more teams overtook us (having also become alive to the necessity for haste) and every night for some time other teams caught up with us until we were about forty souls in all.

Mr. Evenson and I finally selected a location for our sawmill and after considerable hardship reached the top of the divide between Bevin's and Ramshorn Gulches on December 7, where we went into temporary camp, with no shelter beyond that afforded by a large spruce tree. As the snow was getting deep and there was no feed for stock, I started the next morning for Virginia City (18 miles distant) with the cattle, hoping to sell them; but finding no buyer I started to take them out to the ranch of an acquaintance twenty-five miles down the Stinking Water. On the way I was held up and robbed by the notorious George Ives and Irving. After I had complied

MANCHESTER MILL ON FIVE MILE CREEK near The Dalles, Oregon, 1912. (Photo G. E. Manchester)

HADLOCK SAWMILL in Washington's early days. (Photo University of Washington)

with Mr. Ives command to hand him my purse, I was ordered to drive on. He still held his revolver in his hand, which looked suspicious to me, so in speaking to my team I quickly turned my head and found that he had his revolver leveled at me, taking sight at my head. Instantly I dodged as the shot went, receiving the full force of the unexploded powder in my face — the bullet passing through my hat and hair. It stunned me for an instant, and as I staggered against the near leader, accidentally getting my arm over his neck, which prevented me from falling. Almost at once I regained my senses and faced Ives who had his pistol lowered but raised it with a jerk, pointing it at my breast. I heard the click of the hammer but it missed fire. I ran around the oxen, which became very much excited, and my coming in a rush on the other side scared them still more and they rushed against Ives' horse, which in turn got in a tangle with Irving's horse, and during the confusion I struck out for some beaver dams which I noticed close by; but the men soon got control of their horses, and to my agreeable surprise started off in the opposite direction. What had apparently changed their purpose was the sight which also now met my eyes, that of a man driving a horse team who had just appeared over the hill and was now near us. I learned afterwards that Ives and Irving had stopped at Laurin, about two miles from where they overtook me, where Ives fired five shots at the bottles on the shelves because the bartender refused them whisky which accounted for the fact that only one charge was left in his revolver.

But I am getting away from the lumbering subject so I am going back to the camp where Mr. Evenson, the next day, disfigured my face badly in extracting the powder. So with my face bandaged up, in the cold and snow, we managed to build a brush road on grade around a steep mountain to our mill location on the creek. We made a hand sled with cross beams extending outside the runners, so when necessary with a hand spike on each side we were able to nip it along.

With this hand sled we removed our outfit to the creek and we did all the logging this way during the entire winter. We first built a cabin and a blacksmith shop but this became more of a machine shop for when we came to erect the sawmill we met with what seemed unsurmountable difficulties. As I knew nothing about a sawmill I had left the purchase of the outfit to Mr. Evenson, who claimed to be a millwright by profession, but it developed that he had either been very careless in inspecting this machinery or he had not understood it, for so much of it was missing that it seemed impossible to get a working mill out of the material at hand. As there was no foundry or machine shop in this part of the country we were at a loss to know what to do but were determined to erect a sawmill of some kind; so out of our rubber coats and whipsawed lumber we made a blacksmith bellows, then we burned a pit of charcoal, while a broad axe driven into a stump served as an anvil. Mr. Evenson knew a little about blacksmithing so I began to feel somewhat at ease but soon discovered what seemed to be the worst obstacle yet. This was that we had no

"BIG MILL"—SISSON Original mill on site of present Mt. Shasta Pine Manufacturing Co. First operated in '80s by Bernard, Wallbridge and Huntington, then sold to Leland, Wood and Sheldon. Note wooden tram rails and slab conveyor to open fire. (Photo Kaymore Studio courtesy Siskiyou County Historical Society)

gearing for the log carriage, not even the track irons or pinion — and to devise some mechanism that would give the carriage the forward and reverse movement, became the paramount problem. After a great deal of thought and experimenting we finally succeeded in inventing a device which years later was patented and widely used under the name of "rope feed." Incidentally we found this to be such an excellent appliance that we later used it on most of our portable mills, and I have been informed that several manufacturers used and recommended this, charging an additional $300 for it on small mills.

However, in order to construct this, we had to first build a turning lathe and when we came to turn iron shafting, it took much experimenting before we learned to temper the chisels. To turn the shafting (which we made out of iron wagon axles) Evenson would hold the chisel and I with a rawhide strap wrapped around the shafting, taking hold with one hand on each end of the strap, would give a steady, hard pull with the right hand, until the left touched the shaft, then reverse, repeating the process.

These were strenuous days and we worked early and late in the face of the most discouraging circumstances. We manufactured enough material for the sixteen-foot overshot waterwheel, the flume, etc. As we were short of belting, we made it out of untanned oxhides and it worked well enough in the start. We finally got the mill started and sawed about 5000 feet of lumber before we ever had a beast of burden in the camp.

Now as the mill had been tried and proven satisfac-

tory, a crew employed and the mill started, I felt at ease as I imagined all obstacles had now been overcome, so I left the mill and went to Nevada City, a flourishing camp three miles below Virginia City, and opened a lumber yard.

When the lumber commenced arriving from the mill it was disposed of as fast as it landed. When we began selling lumber we made only two grades, sluice or flume lumber which we sold at $140 per M and building lumber (including waney edge) for which we got $125 per M, in gold dust. The demand for lumber was greater than the supply and quite often some of the larger mining companies would send a spy out on the road in order that they might be informed when a load of lumber was approaching. Then they would have a crew of men arrive at the yard simultaneously with the load, and when the team stopped, without consulting me at all, they would unload the lumber and carry off every board to their mines. Soon a man would come along to me with the pay and they always settled according to the bill of lading at the established price so that no loss was incurred by this summary method of marketing our product. Some time after this we also started a yard at Virginia City.

But this prosperous business soon came to standstill for rainy weather set in and the untanned belting began to stretch from the damp atmosphere until it could no longer be kept on the pulleys, so the mill had to be closed down. We heard of a man at Bannack, eighty miles from Nevada City, who had eighty feet of six-inch two-ply belting and we decided to try to get this. Partly by

RAINBOW MILL at head of Box Canyon on headwaters of Sacramento River in Siskiyou County, Calif., owned by Wood and Sheldon in early 1900s. (Photo Kaymore Studio courtesy Siskiyou County Historical Society)

walking and partly by riding a very poor excuse for a horse I found the owner and tried to purchase the belting. No price seemed to attract him, and I finally offered him my entire wealth, consisting of $600 in gold dust — equal to $1200 in currency — but he would not consider the offer. Six-inch two-ply belting would be worth 30 cents a foot in Helena at the present time, or a total of $24 for this piece. Failing to get this belting, I returned to Virginia City, where I learned of a man who owned some canvas which I succeeded in purchasing. I got a saddler to stitch it by hand and this made a very good and efficient belt for our purpose.

Everything was now moving along smoothly with the exception that the head sawyer got killed by coming in contact with the circular saw, and another man was also killed by getting in front of a rolling log on the side of the mountain.

Three miles across the divide was the flourishing mining camp of Bevin's Gulch. The gulch was rich in gold but short of water for mining, so at a miner's meeting of about five hundred men, resolutions were passed to take the water of Ramshorn Gulch, and it did not take long before they had the ditch constructed, taking the water out above the sawmill, leaving the creek dry. Without water we were forced out of business, but the miners needed more lumber, so they agreed to turn in the

water to get the required amount of lumber sawed. When this was going on I was busy getting out an injunction and had to see to it that the sheriff got it served before they again got possession of the water, but the miners, depending upon the strength of their organization, disregarded the order of the court and again turned the water into their ditch and the mill again shut down. As they had left an armed guard at the head of the ditch we had to again appeal to the court. This resulted in the sheriff and some deputies arresting the guard for contempt of court. About a dozen miners were convicted. We obtained a judgment for a few thousand dollars damages, of which only a part were collected, and there was no more attempt to deprive us of the water.

During this year Cover and McAdow started a steam sawmill on Granite Gulch and started a yard at Virginia City. This was then the best mill in the territory. Without any understanding in regard to prices of lumber, they were maintained and business went along satisfactorily, but we wanted more and better machinery, so we agreed that Evenson should go East to purchase a portable steam sawmill, with planing, shingle and lath machinery. He started by stage and stopped at Denver, and apparently having forgotten what he went for, he purchased some oxen and wagons, loaded principally with flour and nails and a primitive planing mill. On his return he got as far as Snake River, Idaho, when he was snowed in, leaving the outfit in charge of strangers. Being refused passage on the stage, he made himself a pair of skiis and took a streak across the mountains for Virginia City, arriving at my office in a fearful snowstorm, without having seen a human being since leaving Snake River.

The stage on which he had been refused passage arrived three days later. Many of the cattle perished and considerable of the merchandise disappeared. What was left was shipped to Virginia City in the early spring of 1865 by pack train at 30 cents per pound freight. It consisted of two kegs of tenpenny nails and 26 sacks of flour. I disposed of the nails at $150 per keg and the flour at $100 per sack, all in gold dust.

During Mr. Evenson's absense I heard of a quartz mill at Bannack which had a portable boiler and engine in it, and as the mill was a failure I thought it might be for sale, so I struck out on horseback the second time. I found the owner and was very much pleased to find a man entirely different from the man who had the eighty feet of belting for he wanted to sell.

I accompanied him to his mill where I inspected his engine. It was a portable Lawrence Machine Co. boiler and engine, cylinders 10 inches in diameter, 12-inch stroke. His price was $1200 which I paid him in gold dust. (Two years later I was offered $6000 for the same engine and refused to sell.)

During the winter of 1864-1865, when we had decided to remove the portable sawmill to Helena (then called Last Chance), as the engine and boiler needed repairs, we looked about us for means of doing what was needed. Machine work was required but as there were no machinists to be had in those days, we had to content ourselves with the help of two blacksmiths who seemed to be willing to do what they could. I had made arrangements to meet them in Nevada City and I started from Virginia City with a load of supplies, including a 125-pound anvil — of which more later — and a team of mules. When I reached Nevada City the men had not appeared and it seemed expedient to return to Virginia City and hunt them up. Realizing that the team had a hard day's work ahead, I thought it best to walk back and found them sitting comfortably over a fireplace. They demurred at going with me, saying it was too cold and stormy but they finally accompanied me to Nevada City from where we started on our way. For the first six miles we had good sleighing but when we got through the canyon the snow gave out so we could ride no further. When we reached Bevin's Gulch the snow was so deep that we still had to walk as it was all the team could do to pull the sleigh and load of supplies. Indeed in many places the load had to be removed, and when the sled was gotten through the drift, the load carried over and reloaded. This was not so bad except for the aforesaid anvil which seemed to get very heavy by the time I had carried it over all the big drifts in the gulch. My men would not assist me any in this work so I was getting pretty well exhausted. To add to my fatigue and discomfort, the lines were too short to permit me to walk behind the sled and drive so I had to struggle through the snow beside the sled.

Finally, after dark, we reached the mining camp of Bevin's and I found a place where I could rest the mules for the night and give them the feed I had carried. I was very anxious to reach the mill that night but the men refused to go any farther with me and the team could not go on. I had been keeping at this place a pair of skiis for us to use in getting to the mill, but someone had "borrowed" them so I had to set out on foot. I had eaten nothing since early morning and was rather exhausted. I got on well enough for part of the way but soon the snow was so deep I would have to lie down on it, press it down as much as possible, then walk a few

"TAKE 'EM AWAY!" This is what the sawdust stiff saw after he'd blown her in on the skidroad? Actually these snakes were collected on Link River, Ore., while feeding on migrating frogs —probably by some unemployed photographer. (Charles Miller Collection Collier State Park Logging Museum)

LAST WORD IN 1900 SAWMILLS was this new plant of Weed Lumber Co., Weed, Calif. Still operating after 57 years. (Photo Tingley Collection Collier State Park Logging Museum)

steps and repeat the process. It got so I could only go a rod or two without resting. I began to imagine I heard voices around me and among them I recognized those of some of my childhood's playmates and that of my mother who was still living.

Then a new danger confronted me. In resting an almost irresistible impulse to sleep would possess me, but having experience in this direction before, realized that if I gave way to it, the sleep would be my last, so with almost superhuman effort I would get on my feet again and go on. Finally I reached the divide where there was almost half a mile of practically level ground with little snow. Slowly my senses seemed to return and the sound of voices ceased. I had now come about two miles and had only about a mile more to go so I commenced to regain hope that I would reach the mill. Hard blasts of wind would strike me now and then and felt as though they were passing through my body. I encountered a few drifts but managed as before to get through them. Then getting to the down grade towards the mill, I found the snow too deep for me on the wagon grade so I attempted to go straight for the mill, but the slope of the mountain was very steep and, not having sufficient strength left to keep up the mountainside I was beginning to have a desperate struggle to get there. I encountered a good many fallen trees and now was so weak that where it was possible I crawled under the trees instead of over them to save strength.

I finally got to the creek about a third of a mile below the mill where there was a deserted cabin. The snow was very deep and fortunately I found a board about ten inches wide and fourteen feet long. So I took

this and laid it on the snow and crawled its length, then pulled it along, and repeated the process until I finally reached the mill cabin. The snow was shoveled away for a distance from the door and I took quite a little rest on the snowbank from where I could look in through the window and see a brisk fire burning in the fireplace. I laid there and planned how I could get strength to walk in and reach a stool that I could see in front of the fire. I did not want to make any disturbance and wake up the men sleeping in the cabin and it seemed almost impossible to again get on my feet, but I felt sleep overcoming me again, so I made another start and got to the woodpile in front of the door, where I fell, and again almost went to sleep. This warned me so I made an effort to reach the door, grasped the latch with my left hand, opened the door and stepped in. I tried to get hold of the inside of the door and close it, but I dropped on the floor, when Evenson who was sleeping in the room, awoke, and rushed to assist me. The men sleeping in the other part of the cabin now awoke and naturally supposing me to be frozen, they all rushed to my assistance. They soon had mittens, boots and socks off but found that while my clothes were frozen stiff on the outside, they were damp with perspiration on the inside. I knew that I was not frozen so asked to be let alone as all I needed was rest and some food. Soon they gave me a dish of cold boiled beef — all the food to be had at that time, as there were no vegetables or flour in that part of the country. I remember that I thought that never had anyone enjoyed such luxury as I lying on the floor in front of the fire, and weakly trying to eat the cold beef. After a time they put me on the bed, stripped me and gave me a brisk rubbing with rough towels, then put on some warm dry clothing, covered me up and left me to sleep and recover from my exhaustion. Being very strong and having great recuperative powers, strange as it may seem, the next morning, although I felt quite rocky, I was able to get about, and I got on some skis, and accompanied by some of the mill hands, went back to Bevin's, hitched up the mules and drove back to Virginia City, reaching there the same evening without further trouble.

A man that I will call Van for short, already had a lumber yard started in Helena. His sawmill was a water power mill, about the same style as our Ramshorn mill. He was selling building lumber at $100 per M. I had heard of him before as the wealthiest man in Montana. I happened to meet Mr. Van on my first day in Helena. He was quite abusive and told me that the lumber business belonged to him, as he was there first, and wanted me to move my mill somewhere else, and said if I did not he would reduce the price of lumber down to $40 per M if necessary.

The freight outfit that had been left at Snake River finally arrived with the empty wagon and the long-looked-for planing mill. It was a primitive looking machine. The frame was made of pine lumber and the feed gearing looked very delicate, but we put it up and by having one man to pull and another to push to help the feed gearing when passing the boards through the machine, we got along fairly well as we were getting $40 per M extra for surfacing and matching. I sometimes became disgusted but when strolling about the premises there was some satisfaction in realizing that I was part owner of the first engine and boiler that ever turned a wheel in Montana. The portable engine and boiler, twenty-five or thirty horse-power, had been shipped from St. Louis to Fort Benton in the spring of 1862 by the American Fur Co. I was also part owner of the first sawmill, a part of which was made at Pike's Peak and completed at Ramshorn, Montana, and last but not least, the planer and matcher, also made at Pike's Peak.

Mr. Van had already started to drive us out of business. He kept the price up but privately allowed large discounts for cash. I had no time to give Mr. Van my attention, for I had to get back to Virginia City to get the Ramshorn mill started. On my arrival at Virginia City I learned I was reported to have left the territory for parts unknown.

This news had already reached the mill and some of the employees had arrived in town and seemed highly pleased to see me. They did not appear to need their money as much as they imagined, and all of them wanted to go back to work, but one man, and he had $400 due him and wanted to return to the states. I succeeded in borrowing this amount from one Mr. Brown, then doing a sort of banking business, but when I saw the kind of gold dust he was going to let me have, it was so poor that I had to object to the quality. I went after my man

and told him that the dust was poor but he was satisfied with it after he examined it. I gave my note for thirty days with interest at 10 percent per month, in bankable gold dust, that is, gold dust free from black sand and adulteration, worth at least 20 per cent more than the kind loaned.

I soon returned to Helena and the sawmill, and learned from Mr. Benton that Mr. Van had dropped prices $10 at a time until lumber was now selling at $60 per M, with a discount of $10 per M, so Mr. Van was doing a good business and getting the money, while we were getting the credit and collections were not sufficient to pay running expenses. There was a good demand for building lumber in Helena at this time so I concluded to pass by Mr. Van. I instructed my yard man to reduce the price of building lumber from $60 to $40 and to allow no credit.

I then went to the sawmill where I had a consultation with the employees and loggers who were supplying logs on a contract. I informed them of my instructions to the yard man and told them I wanted to keep the sawmill running, and told the loggers to get in all the logs they possibly could before winter as there would be no feed for the stock. I wanted the mill operated to its full capacity but would not remove any more lumber from the mill than could be sold for cash, surplus to be stacked at the mill.

I had bought out my partner Evenson's interest in June and allowed him to take the cash on hand, so the only promise I could make in the way of salaries was to supply them with the necessities of life until the lumber could be disposed of; so I had a roll call and told them to answer "yes" if they cared to remain and "no" if they did not care to work on this basis. Every man answered "yes."

The next day I returned to Virginia City where the mill had gotten started and business was in pretty good shape. I then returned to Helena after an absence of about two weeks. The man in charge of the yard told me what lumber there was in the yard was sold and paid for and that he could not get from the mill fast enough to supply the demand; also that Mr. Van had quit shipping lumber to Helena. I took the money on hand in the office and went to the mill. I met the men after supper time and after ascertaining the amount wanted, I told them that it amounted to less than half of what I had expected they would need, and they could double up just as well as not, as it was as convenient for me to pay now as it would be any other time; but they had all they wanted. However it had the effect of establishing confidence.

I spent the greater part of the summer at Virginia City and Ramshorn, taking my brother M. M. Holter in as partner, adopting the firm name — A. M. Holter & Bro. In the fall I left my brother in charge at Virginia City and moved to Helena.

ECHOES FROM THE SPOKANE PINES

The timbered hills of Eastern Washington, threaded by bubbling creeks which flowed into the Spokane River, looked good to the Graham family. They had migrated long miles from Ottawa, Kansas, in 1888, and settled at Windsor, a short distance from Spokane Falls. The Graham brothers built a sawmill here but when they got the job of furnishing timbers for the first Monroe Street bridge in the Falls, they moved their equipment to the north bank of the Spokane River. With this move, Charlie Graham and his brothers started a sawmill dynasty which in its limited way was to become a vital growth factor in the Spokane area.

By 1890 the Grahams wanted to homestead and went northeast 50 miles to the Scotia district, building another sawmill up the Little Spokane. This was later sold to Solomon Wigle who operated it for many years. Charlie Graham took his little family about three miles down river and built his own waterwheel sawmill, producing 12 to 15 thousand feet of white pine, tamarack, cedar and fir each ten hour day and selling it for about $8 a thousand.

Lumbering in the area was good as the city of Spokane was rapidly expanding and waterpower not good enough for the Grahams. About 1910 they rebuilt the Scotia mill and powered it with steam so they could slab out timbers and ties for the Great Northern Railway then coming through Newport and for the Division Street bridge in 1915, which collapsed soon after. In later years Charlie's sons — Bud, Dutch and Jim, worked in the mill crew.

Meanwhile another family in the vicinity had taken to sawmilling. Ferdinand Beyersdorf, with his wife, five sons and a daughter, had traded Missouri for Washington in 1899, at first operating a small mill in the Cheney-Spangle area then in 1901 moving to Milan. In 1903 this mill was moved to Bailey's Lake and enlarged, operating until 1907. This sawmilling start was strictly a Beyersdorf family enterprise in which the men gained valuable experience for later full-scale operations. One of these was the Wild Rose Prairie mill.

Fire was a continual menace in the dry area. Sparks from passing trains or waste piles enflamed the parched mill buildings and played havoc with the countryside

SPOKANE RIVER POWERED GRAHAM MILL Charles Graham, whose father pioneered in sawmilling at Windsor, homesteaded and built this waterwheel and mill in 1900 at what is now Scotia, above Spokane. 5 men took 12 to 15 thousand feet out of mill in 10 hour day. (Photo courtesy Doris Schaub)

GRAHAM STEAM MILL—SCOTIA, WASHINGTON Successor to the waterpower mill Charlie Graham built here in 1895. Furnished timbers for Great Northern when it came through Newport area and for Spokane's first Division Street bridge. Mill was later destroyed by fire starting from slab burner. (Photo courtesy Doris Schaub)

SAWING PINE AT MEAD—1930s in another Graham mill, 7½ miles north of Spokane. At levers is Cress Beyersdorf, one of leaders in his family's sawmill enterprises at Milan, Bailey's Lake, Wild Rose Prairie and Diamond Lake. Beyersdorf had married Alice Graham, daughter of Charlie Graham, sawmilling pioneer in the area. Donor of this s e r i e s of photographs is their daughter. (Photo courtesy Doris Schaub)

settlements and timber. One such fire, starting on August 10, 1910, ended in bitter tragedy. Several small fires in the Sacheen Lake area combined their malevolence to sweep through parts of 54 thousand acres, taking four lives and leaving hundreds homeless, with resulting timber losses of many thousands.

The Beyersdorf mill at Wild Rose Prairie was one of the bases of operation for the fire fighters. The big cook house and bunkhouse could feed and sleep a lot of men. There were day and night fire crews and round-the-clock meals, the coffee pot always ready.

Doris (now Mrs. Schaub), daughter of Cress Beyersdorf who was one of the five sons and had married Alice Graham, well remembers her mother telling about the great columns of smoke pluming up on each side of the

settlement at Scotia. "It was a terrifying time for everybody. In the night the fire started its steady ascent of the hills around us, the sky lighted up for miles. When the flames began coming down toward our homes, the men packed children and wives into wagons and took them all to the Scotia hotel while they went back to the mill and back-fired to stop the flames. This had to be done at night while the air was still and the heat bearable. The families eventually came home, the smoke still so heavy the sun couldn't be seen for days. When it finally did become visible, Charlie Graham sighed: "There's a twenty dollar goldpiece."

There was another big fire in this same Scotia district in 1920. Charlie Graham had a mill out on the Stateroad then which was in a direct path of the fire.

ROUGH LUMBER FOR SPOKANE was hauled by wagons from this Milan, Washington, mill on the Pratt place, 1902. This was a Beyersdorf mill, operated by Ferdinand and his five sons—Lafe, Fred, Cress, Walter and Guy. Out of this crude beginning grew the larger sawmills in Deer Park and Diamond Lake areas. (Photo courtesy Doris Schaub)

BAILEY'S LAKE MILL—1902 to 1907, owned by Beyersdorf family. Son Cress said: "That lake's so big you can hardly spit across it." (Photo courtesy Doris Schaub)

THEY ICED THE ROADS WITH A "RUTTER" so sleighs like this could ride on a hard surface. Beyersdorf men plowed trail through snow with heavy "rutter," 24 feet long with two sets of runners. 500 gallon barrels of water were carried along trail and icy road formed. On steep grades, "sand monkey" rode sleighs. (Photo courtesy Doris Schaub)

WILD ROSE PRAIRIE MILL did thriving business in 1907-1910. This Beyersdorf mill was managed by son Fred. Band saws cut 50 thousand feet a day and kept 300 men busy in woods, camps, mill and cookhouse. Mill facilities used by fire fighting crews during "black days" but mill was later moved because of fire hazards. (Photo courtesy Doris Schaub)

Everything burned within a few feet of the mill. Charlie was smoke blind for a couple of weeks and was doctored in the good old fashioned way with "tea leaf poltices." The Beyersdorf mill at Diamond Lake was also threatened by this fire with the families being evacuated to nearby Newport for safe keeping.

Stories are told about both fires concerning the burying of their dishes and other valuables. Mrs. Schaub's aunt said they even planned on burying the piano if the fire got too close.

There were also the quieter times in the rugged pioneer life. One of the women says: "There was nothing behind those rough lumber houses but miles of wilderness. We had only feeble kerosene lamps — no inside water or plumbing. The latter was usually down a path that seemed miles long in the dark. We had to carry water for washing, lugging it up from the river to fill the copper boilers on the cook stoves. Washing clothes was a full day's job without any thanks. Then another long day ironing, the flat irons 'het up' on the ranges. There were weeks of canning too. Winter? Well, the community was usually snowed in. People visited back and forth and had quilting bees, pinochle parties or listened to the champion fiddler play "Arkansas Traveler," "Chicken Reel" and "Old Zip Coon."

The last sawmill operated by the Beyersdorf clan was the largest — at Diamond Lake. Fred was the manager, Cress the sawyer. They cut 100 thousand feet every 24 hours. The cookhouse was an institution. Cress tells of the big French head cook who swung a carving knife

BIGGEST BEYERSDORF PRODUCER was this Diamond Lake operation. Cookhouse was a notable establishment, ruled by a French cook and carving knife. Cress Beyersdorf was sawyer and said: "The Hunkies and Bohunks ate up everything in sight like a swarm of locusts. We had to put them by themselves and water the milk 3 to 1". (Photo courtesy Doris Schaub)

CREW OF GRAHAM MILL—1915 Second from left is Charlie Graham who built and operated mill. Two standing together in center are sons Bud and Dutch. (Photo courtesy Doris Schaub)

WHEN BUTTER WAS 15 CENTS and you paid your bill with a hog. Charlie and Oscar Stangland ran this store in Scotia and sold calico, coffee beans and cordwood. (Photo c o u r t e s y Doris Schaub)

if anybody complained that the mutton was goat or the coffee part hay. He remembers the untractable Bulgarian and Hungarian "bohunks" who "ate up everything in sight like locusts descending on a harvest and drank great pitchers of milk. The other men growled so much we had to set up separate tables for our Baltic guests and water their milk 3 to 1. Lucky for them we needed men — tough, hard workers, used to hardships like they were."

And the general store at Scotia — full of pungent smells and gossip just as spicy. Owned by Charlie and Oscar Stangland (and in later years by Sol Wigle) it carried everything from kerosene to dried apples, from pillow tops to barn hinges. Calico was 10 cents a yard, coffee beans 15 cents a pound. You took these home and ground them in your own mill. Flour sold for 80 cents a hundred. If you had eggs and made butter at home you traded them for black strap molasses and soda biscuits. If you had to buy eggs, they were expensive — 10 cents a dozen.

Because Scotia was on the G. N., supplies were brought up from Spokane on the train for the store at Scotia and also the sawmill-owned store at Diamond Lake 3½ miles distant.

The Beyersdorf and Graham mills were part of an era, furnishing material for much of the Inland Empire. They were the focal point of the saga of two family dynasties stemming from plains pioneers to builders of the New West.

SAWMILLING AT SILVERTON — 1890

In 1890 a mill owned and operated by Matthias Johnson was moved to a spot nine miles southeast of Silverton. The Johnson mill was a circular saw type with two saws and a planer. It was operated by steam power and had an average cut of perhaps 7000 feet.

No effort was made to make this mill convenient or handy. It had no cut off saw, and slabs for making steam were cut with an ax wielded by the engineer who was also the fireman. Logs were turned on the carriage with a large wooden friction bull-wheel and a small drum around which wound a rope with a hook on the end. If the wheel failed to turn the log, men came with peavies and supplemented the wheel power. A wheelbarrow with a large box on it was used for hauling away sawdust, and the offbearer probably had never heard of such things as live rolls.

Mr. Johnson, the owner and also the sawyer, and six men comprised the crew. A workday was ten hours and the pay for common labor $1.50 per day, without board. The bullwhacker received $2.50, the engineer and the offbearer $2 each per day. Some of the men walked from their homes a mile or more away and one came two miles. The only way one could know whether or not the mill would run was to be on hand at seven o'clock each morning. If it did not operate one could return home and wait one, two or three days or possibly a week before receiving word to report for work. There were no telephones.

The mill crew were frequently called on to go into the woods as loggers. If no logs were cut the mill closed down and all hands repaired to the woods to cut a supply. They sometimes felled and bucked logs two or three days; then they would start the mill and saw the logs into lumber while the bullwhacker continued, with three yoke of oxen, to deliver logs at the mill.

Most of the lumber, except flooring, ceiling, rustic and lumber of this class, was cut on orders so logs were bucked the proper length and knowing what was wanted, the men had some idea of what sort of trees to fall. If clear was wanted an old soft grained yellow fir was selected. If flooring mostly was needed a hard grained tree was chosen while for rough lumber any tree, not too rough, was taken. If the order was for clear timber rough trees were not cut, but if the order was for rough lumber, only trees which would make rough was cut and those which indicated a high percentage of clear were not molested.

Grading was a simple matter. But two grades were considered and those only for clear. No. 1 clear, allowed no serious defects and no knots more than one foot from the end. No. 2 clear was all that did not meet the requirements of No. 1.—F. H. Hadley in Four L Bulletin June, 1924.

KLAMATHON MILL—1889 TO 1902 which had brief but colorful career as outlet for logs from famous Pokegama Chute. Full story is told by Eugene S. Dowling in Siskiyou County Historical Yearbook for 1948. (Photo Kaymore Studio courtesy Siskiyou County Historical Society)

DRAMA IN THE SUGAR PINE

With the Pokegama Chute at the mountain end and the Klamathon mill down the Klamath River, enough drama was packed into the ten years from '92 to '02 to last most mill enterprises fifty. This turn of the century activity took place on Oregon's southern front where the Klamath crosses into California.

Actually the story begins in 1889 when the Klamath River Lumber and Improvement Co. began construction of a sawmill and surveyed a townsite for Klamath City on the bare slopes extending down to the river from Black Mountain. The project also included a log dam and wagon bridge. But all this was washed out by high water in 1890.

In the fall of '91, about the time the new Southern Pacific Railroad crossed the Klamath River, the John R. Cook interests set up the Pokegama Sugar Pine Co., purchased the townsite and completed the mill. On July 23 of the next year it was sawing, using logs driven down river from the Pokegama Chute and held in booms by cribs stretched across the river weighted by rocks. (Photographs and description of the logging and chute opera-

tion are given in the forerunner to this book, "Glory Days Of Logging.")

The Pioneer Box Factory, established by Sacramento money and located near the Klamathon mill, was subsequently purchased by the John Cook interests, which in 1897 leased the mill to Hervey Lindley. Rafts of lumber were floated down the raging Klamath, a precarious operation at best. About 10 thousand feet was chained together, floating with about 5″ above water. Four or five men rode on top of the load, working long sweeps to keep the raft off rocks and banks at river bends. Trouble usually occurred at Lime Gulch, below the mouth of Humbug Creek, where rafts were broken up and the men having to swim for it.

But the disaster which ended the "short, happy life" of the Pokegama Sugar Pine Co. was the big fire. At midnight, October 13, 1902, flames whipped by a savage wind, completely destroyed the mill, box factory, 8 million feet of lumber, 25 business buildings and many residences in the town. The mill was never rebuilt.

THEY DID IT THE HARD WAY Whip or pit sawing before the turn of the century. Saw was pulled and pushed by men above and below pole trestle. The big trick was to get the log on the platform. This method was used in California in the '80s and '90s, in Alaska as late as 1905. (U.S. Forest Service photo from W. C. Lumbermen's Association)

WHEN SAWMILLING WAS TWO-HANDLED

There wasn't much glamor to whipsawing lumber but there was wages in it. California and Oregon miners needed timbers and boards for shaft props, sluice boxes, their shacks, flumes and always a board laid across a couple of nail kegs. One of the first things the westward ho pioneers did when they stopped for the last time was to get out their whipsaws, axes, wedges and mauls and go to work. And there's a story told about the miner who dug a whipsaw pit and panned $600 out of the diggings.

What was this whipsawing process like — this early attempt at sawmilling? Actually it made use of two saw forms — the simple whip saw and the pit frame saw. A pit was dug or trestles built on the flat ground. The log was squared with a broadaxe and placed over the

pit or on the trestles, one man straddling or standing on the log (topman), the other working underneath it (pitman). The saw was six to eight feet long, ends fitted with tiller-type handles. When saw line was chalked on the log the two men pulled and pushed, cutting on the downward stroke only. A good day's work by this back-breaking process was 200 lineal feet for which in 1850 they got 20 to 30 cents a foot.

The pit frame saw was thinner and better adapted to hardwood or where waste in sawdust was a cost factor. Each end of the saw was attached to a wooden frame by iron shackles. Wedges could be driven into a slot at the lower end to draw the blade tight. This frame saw was the forerunner of the muley or sash saw used in most water power mills.

GULLET CRACKS

by RALPH W. ANDREWS

A Story of a Sawmill Feud reprinted from
Adventure Magazine, May, 1928

If you're a sawmill man you'll snort and if you're not you won't know what it means but Matt McKie loved band saws. He wasn't like most mill men there. He wasn't always smarting under the whip of the screeching, whining, gutting things—beaten down but still sweating on the job on pay day. The saws didn't tear through his tough, gruel-fed soul, because they knew him for their friend. Yes, sir, Matt McKie was different and he loved those saws of his with a passion that flamed continually even though the heat of it was never fanned by love returned.

Matt was a filer in Douglas fir country but he never saw a band saw as some fire-eating thing gashing bitterly into the tough fibres of the log. Laugh if you want to but Matt McKie—big, red-necked, blue eyed Matt—helped drag those sixty foot endless bands, hot and limp, into the filing room as if they were mischievous airedales worn out after a morning's play, ready to be petted and have their ears scratched by the swage dies.

A fellow like that ought to get along, liking his work as much as that. And he'd be a good filer. Matt was. The Ridge Run mill, which for most purposes was Kramer, the general superintendent, wouldn't have acknowledged any man a better filer. Matt didn't get much money but Matt didn't care for much money. What was money to a man who could imagine the wolfdog howl of a sawdust-thirsty band saw as the playful bark of some scampering pup? Kramer understood Matt and humored him. But the men . . .

"Matt McKie? You mean Mutt McKie — that big hunk of hoot-mon Scotchman? Say — any guy with soft feelin's for a cussed piece of steel is headed for the bone pile. He's cracked!"

Cracked, eh? Well, if he was, his saws didn't get that way very often — very often. They did once in a while. The throats of his panting little pets got choked up with sawdust sometimes and came in from play with a few half-inch cracks down in their gullets. And how Matt did hate a gullet crack. He could jam his finger or break a swage lever or bang his squash-shaped head on the T-bar of the saw rack and go on humming "A Hundred Pipers" contentedly but just let a saw develop some gullet cracks and he didn't sleep until he knew the why of them.

Cracked or not, Matt liked his job and loved his saws. And cracked or not, the men laughed and flung gibes at him, and when he didn't pay any attention to them, they thought he was dead on his feet. But Matt went along, fondling and scratching the backs of his charges, not caring much what they thought. He'd have kept right on that way too, chewing his fine cut and humming old country ballads, if those jagged bullet holes in his nice fresh saw hadn't stared him in the face that morning.

There were a couple of things that led up to the bullet holes. One concerned a fellow who worked on the green chain — a putty-colored young back-country bumpkin named Zevic whom Matt knew. The other was a bunkhouse dare that Matt didn't know about. But Zevic. About two nights before Matt had been lumbering along the plank walk toward the bunkhouse, close on the heels of four others who were smelling corned beef and cabbage and kicking their heels. His coat was draped over his shoulder in spite of the raw March air. Maybe he was still thinking about the creatures he had left in his workshop as his Ayrshire father used to think about the wooden figures he carved. Anyhow he didn't notice Zevic dropping back, yanking the coat loose and rolling it into a ball, booting it into the mud. The coat was ragged and sour-smelling but Matt objected.

Zevic laughed and the others with him laughed.

"Ha, Hoot-mon — where's your coat?"

"Go lay-down with it, Mutt, or whistle it back."

Zevic didn't say a word and he suddenly wished he had left the coat alone. He hadn't been out of the hills very long and at Ridge Run he'd heard the banter the men flung at Matt McKie. Always before this muddle-head had taken it like an easy going draft horse. But now he felt his jumper choking his neck and his head jerked up as though a sledge had tapped his chin. Matt's flushed face jutted forward.

"Is there no manners to ye, witches brat! Pick up that jacket or I'll make a stump out of ye!"

Matt wasn't exactly mad but he fooled Zevic and the onlookers when he sent the yokel spinning backward. It takes a husky to break the spirit of timbers on the green chain but right then Zevic was less husky. There was a ditch running alongside the walk and he slipped into it, stumbling to his knees. Matt followed his advantage and ground a handful of ragweed into the bumpkin's protesting mouth and swiped his coat across the face.

"Now go get your porridge, little mon. And take all these other animals with ye!"

This last was addressed to the disappointed spectators

FIRST IN BEND was this sawmill of Bend Company. Supt. George Gove, at left of log, had come from Cleveland and Hammond Lumber Co. in Mill City in 1911 and stayed in charge when Brooks-Scanlon Lumber Co. took over. (Photo courtesy George Gove)

"LITTLE NORWEGIAN MILL ACROSS THE RIVER" was what Shevlin-Hixon rivals called Brooks-Scanlon's Mill A, successor to Bend Company mill, built in 1916. Mill B was built in 1923 and Brooks-Scanlon bought Shevlin-Hixon interests in 1950. (Photo courtesy George Gove)

BEND FOURTH OF JULY PARADE in 1921 included a dozen new Gerlinger carriers with hard rubber tires and other modern features. (Photo by Ray Van Vleet)

who dodged the coat Matt swung at them. Mill men like a brawl and while this moment Matt McKie had raised his stock with them, they had been railling him too long to admit it.

"Ain't Scotty a tiger when you get his Irish up? Come on, get up — hunky, you with the mouthful of spinach. Why didn't you stand up to him? You could have knocked his head off that red neck!"

Perhaps Zevic could have done just that, and then again perhaps Zevic had other plans brewing. In fact, two mornings later, when Matt McKie had gotten over the first shock of seeing that fresh twelve-inch steel pet of his ruined by the jagged edges of holes that nothing but bullets could have made, he figured Zevic had started working on those plans.

When he had punished him that other night, it had been like spanking a bad boy, but now a fire was burning. Zevic, only Zevic, could have tampered with the thing he loved. Zevic, smarting under the spanking, must have sidestepped the night watchman and put a row of bullets through the saw that was almost a part of Matt McKie. So there was nothing to do but annihilate Zevic.

He looked like a madman bent on destruction, Matt did, when he went stumping stiffly down the cleated incline from the sawing floor, arms swinging like a windmill's fins. The seven o'clock whistle hadn't sounded yet and the mill was quiet, hushed perhaps, in awe of what was about to happen. Two men at the foot of the ramp guessed he was going somewhere in a hurry. It was Zevic who knew where.

The young hillbilly saw him coming. He was up on the working platform of the green chain, relacing his shoe, ready to take up his cant hook when the lumber started coming along the chain. His eyes were a little squinty from the dead sleep of the night but he saw Matt's eyes clear enough and — were those sparks shooting out of them?

He dropped the lacing and scraped to his feet instantly. He might have been watching a mountain still and rising up to defend it from the revenuers, hands spread over his hips, head set on his chest, his whole yellow-topped frame waiting tensely. And then Matt was below him, shaking two fists.

"What spit o' hell are ye, mon! It's foulin' me coat and now me beautiful saw. By the light of the powers — I'll slay ye, I will!"

His arms came over the platform like two jump sparks and his big hands caught Zevic's ankles. The towhead broke his manly pose and tried to leap back out of the steel grip; but it held and Zevic went off balance, sprawling backward on the moving chains. Men were running up.

"Come on, hunky — now's your chance! Get up and knock that knotheaded Scotchman clear over the sawdust burner!"

Zevic got up — almost. Matt was scrambling over the edge of the platform like a bull scaling a river bank. Once up, he lurched his big bulk upon the recovering form. But Zevic was fighting now. He was a bull too, a lighter, more agile young bull. He managed to swing aside until he could straighten himself and then planted a fist in Matt's face. He carried the fight now, hammering at the puffing mouth until Matt had to drop his head and grope for the throat that was never there, his fingers coming away with nothing more than shreds of Zevic's red cotton shirt.

Matt was no fighter. He could never stand up and trade blows. Instinct drove him to the earth and when he succeeded in getting a grip on Zevic's shoulders, he tried to drag him down. But he couldn't. That young husky was facing the mill yard when he saw Kramer coming on a run. He knew the fight was almost over yet his fellow workers kept clamoring for more action and he couldn't ease up. His eyes caught the canthook

BIG LATH CROP Like a farmer driving down rows of corn, Shevlin-Hixon teamster stacks lath in storage yard. (Photo by Ray Van Vleet)

"BURNER COST A MILLION" — it was said in Bend. Big Shevlin-Hixon Lumber Co. mill in Bend, Oregon, with its three stacks and log slips. Burner on the left was over 100 feet high, built of fire brick 4 feet thick and covered with ½ and ⅜ inch steel plate. When mill was abandoned, burner was scientifically dynamited, steel sold to sheep ranchers for use as water tanks. (Photo by Ray Van Vleet)

leaning against the post and he swept it into his hand, clubbing the handle of it squarely into Matt's inflamed face as it came in again. So instead of bringing Zevic down, Matt went down himself. The canthook stopped him short. Blood oozed out between his fingers as he clapped his hand to his mouth like a startled child and slumped to his knees.

"You two yahoos! What the hell's going on?"

That was Kramer, spinning Zevic around. The canthook rattled to the platform.

"This here filer — he says I spoiled some saws or somethin'. It don't make sense. He jumped me and —"

"You, Matt. Straighten up. What's the matter with you?"

"The saw — the fresh saw ready for the wheels!" Matt flourished a bloody paw. "It has holes from bullets in it — Muster Kramer. This mon — he did it. Aye — he did. Chucked me coat in the mud, him. Yes — I roughed him up. Now to get even — he shoots holes in the saw!"

Kramer finally got it straight and Zevic swore by all his Arkansas forefathers that he didn't know anything about it and never had a gun anyway. But work was work and Kramer hustled the crews to their jobs. He sent the filer up to his sanctuary spitting teeth and blood and Gallic curses and he shook Zevic with a warning:

"We'll see what's behind this, you young wildcat! Get to work."

When Kramer beheld the saw he wasn't so sure Matt McKie was wrong. Something was wrong somewhere all right. He'd heard of everything else in a filing room including a milk-bearing cow but a gun! But it sure looked like somebody had a grudge against Matt or the mill. They got a new saw on the band wheels and the filer insisted on brazing a new section into the maimed one. "All right," Kramer agreed. "Turn in overtime and I'll charge it off to labor troubles with thick-headed sawdust stiffs!"

Matt wouldn't charge off anything; the hurt was too deep for that. Not the physical hurt. The canthook had

48

sheared off three teeth and torn his gums and lip but these didn't bother Matt much. But still he dragged himself around the filing room in a dour, unbroken silence. At supper time a man pulled him out behind the cookhouse.

"I'm workin' out in the yard, see? I heard about the fight an' I got to put you wise to somethin'."

Matt McKie only gazed at him dully.

"Your trouble ain't with that young hillpunk, mister. And you ain't liable to guess who it was that shot up that saw because he done it for another reason. It was Jake Wylie, that's who. A bunch of 'em got on a bottle and they had a gun — well, they dared him to pull a bullet through the saw — just to see what you and Kramer would do."

The little lumber stacker backed away cautiously, half expecting more wrath to break forth from Matt's hulking frame. As it was, big Matt only kept on staring blankly.

"That spawn o' hell — Zevic!"

A raw wind whipped up over the Ridge the next day to cool Matt to the point that his teeth hurt him. He began to think and the more he thought, the more his teeth hurt. It was Kramer though who told him to hop the crummy into Herrick to see a dentist. Matt had thought about doing that but now that Kramer had brought it up, he said he wouldn't go. And he didn't, right then. He went back to his place of worship and trued up the arbor of the saw gummer until every blow on the thing felt as though he were pounding his own jaw. That beat him. He caught the train out and felt queerly about something more than three jagged tooth stumps. He could figure what it was.

Matt probably thought he could see that dentist, get the teeth yanked out and be right back with his precious saw pets. But the Herrick dentist had other ideas. The teeth were so sound and firm in spite of the twenty year erosion of Kentucky fine cut they would have to be crowned. Matt wasn't so stubborn in matters he knew nothing about so he gave in. After an hour in the chair he began to feel easier. The whir of the electric drill reminded him of the sawmill and soothed him when he felt the sting of the bit. It also reminded him that the only other filer in the state of Washington, the man who had taught him most of what he knew in bandsawry, Tom Elmers, lived right here in Herrick. He was filing right now in James and Woods mill and Matt wondered how he was getting along.

Tom Elmers brightened when he saw Matt, quickly explained that the devil was riding the log slip and he was about ready to break away at the sound of the whistle.

"Matt — this is the lousiest mill in the world. There ain't a thing right about it. The sawyer couldn't cut hot butter with a jig saw and the saws are a wreck. They don't wash the grit out of the logs and the carriage feed goes haywire every week. And then, of course, I get blamed because the saws don't stand up and they beller like stuck hogs when I yell for new ones. I'm through. Leaving the fifteenth!"

Matt was all sympathy. He shook his head solemnly and poked around the tools like an old maid in another's workbasket.

"The best mill is the one for you, Thamas — not the worst. Maybe I'll scuttle my own job and take this."

"What? You? What's the matter with Ridge Run?"

"It's a fine mill, Tom. Vurra good mill. But I'm no feelin' so good there. It's trouble wi' me, too — but men trouble. Now your kind — I can bludgeon that kind and I'm in the mind to try." He was running his sensitive fingers over the saws on the racks and trying a tension gauge down the sides of them. "Ye-es, I'm in the mind to try."

"Hop to it, then — you old hoot owl. If anybody can put band saws up and keep 'em up, you can. But why you want to pick on a graveyard like this is more than I know. You mean it? All right. We'll go in and see Blakely and tell him you'll work up some saws for a week until he can get somebody else and I'll skip out right tonight. You can stand it for a week maybe."

"A week, sure Thamas. And Thamas — I guess you quit a long time back. Your saws are in bad shape."

"Yeah — like I told you there ain't any use trying. Come on, we'll see the boss."

It looked as though Matt McKie had forgotten all about Ridge Run and Kramer and Zevic. He told this other superintendent he wanted to go to work right away and he did. Blakely had heard of this impassioned Scotchman down at the Ridge and with his reputation, he never questioned Matt's ability to lick the saws into shape — the saws on which Tom Elmers had gone dead. And he chuckled to himself at the thought of the slick one he and Matt were playing on Kramer. It was paying him back for some of the tricks he'd pulled. But there was one thing that worried Blakely some. McKie hadn't said a word about money. All those stories about him must be true.

Meanwhile Matt was on the job. He went to work at three o'clock that afternoon and it was twelve that night when he gently laid down his ball pein hammer and picked his way around the dry kilns to the scattered lights of Herrick. He had rolled and tensioned and swaged and filed but he had a pair of fresh band saws to show for it. And he was already at the bench next morning when Jensen, the head sawyer, swung into the filing room.

"Heard they got a new man. Glad to know you. Say, I'm glad they got rid of that cuss, Elmers. Now maybe we can get the snake out of them saws and get the grade up some."

Matt shook his hand. He didn't say a word then, went right on with his grinding. The sawyer went out wondering what sort of a clam they'd got now. Just when the siren shrieked seven o'clock, he found out. The clam opened. He had the millwright with him.

"Now — the top wheel is out of true and the guide has to be reset. Journals and bearings on both wheels are worn vurra bad. Tam was right. The saw is naugh but trash but we have to use it. The wheels will have to come off."

The millwright blinked but when he decided this was the voice of authority he got his crew working and uncovered a lot more bad spots than Matt had. And the filer worked right along with the crew. Along in midafternoon they had the band mill back together and were sawing.

The battle-scarred old headsaw sang her hymn without a break until the whistle stopped her at six. In three minutes the sawing floor was as silent as a tomb, every man gone. Every man? Not Matt McKie. He was sitting on a bolt keg, swigging cold coffee from a milk bottle, thinking about the saw on the gummer. When the watchman looked in on him he was adjusting the thrust and he departed without a word. This was a new one on him — a filer working night and day. There was nothing like that in his book.

Matt kept on. The gullets of the saw ground out, the points swaged and filed, he fingered the cold cutting edges with the tenderness of a man scratching his dog's ears. He stopped now and then to take a fresh chew or inspect some antiquated piece of equipment with which the filer in this mill was supposed to get along. Once the blazing blueness of the big nitrogen lamp in the mill yard caught his eye and he stared at it as if for the first time he realized it was night and pitch black outside that circle of light.

He looked at his watch and saw it was ten-thirty; he turned back to the saw to be stopped short by a man leveling an automatic pistol at him.

Matt's wits moved slowly. Maybe he could have saved himself and other people a lot of trouble by leaping at the fellow as he had at Zevic. But Matt had never seen a gun from the receiving end before and he didn't know what it was all about. He knew the face. It belonged to the Ridge Run mill — long and lean, the lines set, narrowed eyes hooded by flickering lashes. But Matt remained immobile, in stark wonderment.

"Well?" The lines of the face broke into a hundred little wrinkles. "Here I am — you Scotch dumbbell! You got the first round on me but I'm here to square it up. You ain't runnin' away from me!"

Matt broke his stance, lifting his hands limply in front of him. "Mon — you're daft. I've done you no mite o' harm."

"Don't get humorous, Scotty. I ain't got long to stay. You know the score all right. I'm Wylie — the guy you got fired — you big mutt! All I did was get tanked up and shoot a couple of holes in a saw belongin' to that stinkin' mill. And you —"

"Mon — I fought the beggar Zevic for that!"

"He never did it, you dumbhead! It was me, all right. Them guys put up a ten-spot. I shot up your pretty saw all right. And you knew it was me. Joe Hoff told you and you screamed to Kramer and he yanked me off the job and I cleaned house on Hoff before I wheeled out of there. You're next. You run away from me but it ain't that easy to give Jake Wylie the slip!"

Clear enough, but do you think Matt McKie understood? He just folded his big red face up in a frown and jiggled a hooked finger at Wylie's leathery leer.

"It is a fine story, Mr. Wylie. But Zevic — bad spawn, that. And not a paltry word have I spoken to Mr. Kramer about you. The mon fired you? I will fix it fine when I go back."

"Fix hell! You fixed enough already. And when I get through with you you ain't goin' to feel like fixin' anything but yourself. Stick to that Zevic stuff all you want but I know you got Kramer to fire me. You ain't goin' to be able to work here and you ain't got any job at Ridge Run. Kramer telephoned to Seattle for a new filer this afternoon."

That one drew blood. For the first time Matt really showed interest. The frown clouded into a black scowl and then his cold blue eyes blazed.

"Fouh-mon! What is that you say?"

"I'm tellin' you — meathead! You're yanked, canned, dished and otherwise fired! You ain't got any more job at Ridge Run than I have and you're goin' to have less than that here when I get through. It's time we was gettin' busy, too. See them saws? If a bullet hole in one of 'em hurts you, you're goin' to get mangled up bad now. Get a cold chisel and a hammer!"

Matt was still puzzling over the report of his lost job. The scowl faded like a summer fog and his eyes looked clear through Jake Wylie. Fingers fumbled at the edge of his jumper.

"Hurry up, you yap! Get them tools!"

Wylie stepped forward to brandish the pistol in front of Matt's face, darting back like a rabbit. His sweeping gaze across the workbench caught a box of tools and he dragged it toward him. In the heap he found a cold chisel and thrust it at Matt's chest.

"Get a hammer! I'm in a hurry and I ain't foolin'. You're the guy that hates gullet cracks, ain't you? Well you're goin' to make some pretty ones by hand!"

If there had been any fight in Matt McKie before, it had fled now. He might have been performing some solemn duty, the way be took the chisel and picked up a hammer. That the saws at Ridge Run which he had watched over and worked with so long should now change masters drained every ounce of spirit from him. He felt no ill feeling against Kramer or anybody. He didn't

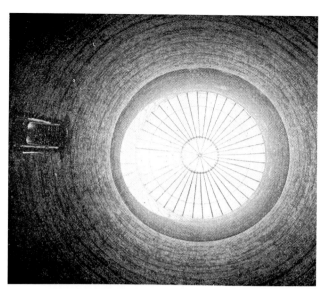

THREE GUESSES Photographer had holiday inside new "million dollar" waste burner at Shevlin-Hixon mill, Bend, Oregon. Camera points upward toward steel screens. Ventilators like the one shown were built into firebrick 4 feet thick. (Photo by Ray Van Vleet)

even seem to notice Wylie, so mechanically did he place the annealed edge of the cold chisel in the gullet of the saw tooth and lift his heavy arm.

Wylie dropped just in time. The heavy ball pein hammer came sweeping with murderous force. But Jake Wylie had dropped like that in pool rooms and the weapon went over his head. Matt didn't press his advantage. Nothing strange about it either. Matt was struck motionless by the roar of that pistol which spit something past his ear to shatter the window behind him. Matt wasn't a fighter and he wasn't used to guns. Jake had hopped to his feet and was bellowing:

"Better not try that again — big boy! I'll show you who's runnin' this carnival. Pick up that chisel and get to workin' on that saw again. The watchman could hear that shot if he was asleep in the boiler room!"

So there was Matt McKie stopping to retrieve the cold chisel. A big, trembling hulk, bending to defeat. Matt McKie — the fallen champion of the band saw. There he was, gazing fixedly at it with Jake Wylie watching like a cat. But he might as well have been a mile away for big Matt was no more than a witless idiot, his protruding eyes wandering from one hand to the other in dumb consternation. For Matt had come from a land where even stern men obey the sterner hand — smarting under it, but in the end obeying. Matt could recognize the authority of a gun. He ran his thumb around the gullet of the vised saw for a moment, finally scraping up the hammer to drive the chisel edge into the quivering steel once more.

"Deeper! Hit it — you muttonhead!"

Deeper went the wound in the tempered metal. Another little gash, another wound in Matt's own flesh.

The hammer blows rang eerily through the silent mill, like the clanking of a prison chain, each one a gouge into a strong man's spirit. And Jake Wylie, grinning through it all, wondering why the watchman didn't show up.

Matt could never have said how long he drove away at that lacerated saw. Another half hour might have passed when he finally came to the end of the flat strip, loosed the vise and slid the saw in its grooves, never looking up. An automatic hand lifted the hammer, another steadied the chisel to meet the blow of the steel head. The hand was lifting again.

"Hey, I thought I heard something like a shot a while ago."

Matt might have been awakening from a bad dream. Wylie was gone. Instead, the watchman's cautious head was thrust through the aperture of the partly open sliding door.

"What you doin' to that saw, for cripes sake!'

Matt wondered too. His eyes rove along the steel band and his fingers felt at the gashes. A startled murderer, touching a lifeless form in unbelief. A deep frown fell over his eyes and then he jerked his head toward the watchman.

But words didn't come — only the hammer slamming down on the chisel as before. Another blow and the V went deeper, the hands moving to the next throat, hands no longer mechanical but propelled by the mind that was. The watchman swung away, his flashlight making a path for his heavily falling feet. Matt listened to those footfalls and when, between blows, he could hear them no more, his whole frame drooped a little and settled to his knees. A clammy hand brushed across his forehead.

Momentarily he got to his feet and drove straight for the door, fumbling, stumbling through the black, hollow mill, down into the chalky blue light of the nitrogen lamp. Beyond the piles of stacked lumber he walked faster, running out upon the rutty road into Herrick.

The last person Kramer could find who had seen Matt McKie was the night watchman and he told Kramer how the big filer was in there hammering away at the saw like a crazy man. The broken window made a deeper mystery of it. Of course nobody knew Jake Wylie had been around. Kramer had fired him that day and forgotten him and then discovered Jake had skipped camp, leaving his wife and kid at the Ridge.

But it wasn't until that letter postmarked Ladysmith, B. C., came along that Kramer and everybody got the picture — after the superintendent had answered it and got Matt to tell the whole story. But that first letter was a masterpiece of Scotch brevity.

"I have a good job here. The mill is good and the people good. Mr. Kramer there was a man there Jake Wylie. I think there is a pay check owing to me. Please I would like you to give it to his widow. I did not know he was married."

(1) Sunnyside Hotel owned by J. R. McInnes. Tub, jug and basin hotel using water from well. Rooms had oil lamps. Sewage went into inlet. In basement was "logger's dancehall." Supplies came by small, oar-propelled scow from Hastings Mill store and were hauled into hotel through trap door in floor. Victoria and Fraser River steamers *Beaver, Grappler* and *Alexander* discharged cargoes of hay, barley, oats, coal, oil, groceries for loggers and surveyors on float—now Union Steamship Dock. They came in at high tide and backed out.

Invisible behind Sunnyside Hotel was Capt. John Deighton's hotel and public house. Newspapers later colored stories about Deighton by referring to him as "Gassy Jack." He was well educated, widely traveled, trustworthy master of Fraser River vessels carrying passengers and gold, was given largest funeral in New Westminster's history.

(2) Customs House—Tompkins Brew customs officer and jailer. Jail and yard invisible behind George Black's cottage. (3) George Black's cottage. Platform where clothes are drying supported toilet over water. The "Laird of Hastings" gave fashionable evening dances in this house. (4) George Black's butcher shop. Swing arm used to raise and lower meats from butcher boat. (5) Granville Hotel — Joseph Mannion, "Mayor" of Granville proprietor. Later alderman, writer, art connoiseur. Lord Lansdowne visited here in 1882. Coal oil street lamp in front served as harbor light. Gastown mail from Hastings Mill store landed on float as were supplies from river boats. Moodyville ferry and sloop *San Juan* tied up here. (6) McKendry's—famous "boot and shoe doctor" with trade as far as Cariboo. McKen-

dry was Gastown's volunteer postmaster. (7) George Brew's restaurant, open when owner not in jail. Brew was former cook at Hastings Mill. Later building-housed Blair's Terminus Saloon.

(8) Gin Tei Hing's wash house and general merchandise store. (9) Wah Chong's laundry. (10) Arthur W. Sullivan's general store. (11) Louis Gold's dry goods store. (12) John A. Robertson's wine and spirit shop—also known as "Pete Donnelly," "Hole In The Wall" Saloon. Dr. Master's office was in small building in front. (13) John Robertson's home. Later was Gold House. (14) Blair's house. (15) Tom Fisher's cottage. (16) "Portugese Joe's" trading post. Actual name Gregoria Fernandez. Rented nets to Indians—traded powder, flour for skins. (17) The Parsonage—Wesleyan Methodist services held by Rev. James Turner for Indians and Kanakas.

THIS WAS GRANVILLE IN 1884 — OPPOSITE HASTINGS MILL on Burrard Inlet. Settlement was unofficially dubbed "Gastown" after Vancouver was founded. It occupied general area of Carrall, Hastings and Cambie Streets. Buildings in photo are on what is now water side of Water Street. Timber at left — Cordova Street; right — Cambie Street. Inscription below is condensed from original made by Major J. S. Mathews, Archivist, City of Vancouver, in 1938. (Photo B.C. Provincial Archives)

BURNER WAS A BEACON Famous Hastings sawmill whose refuse burner showed a welcome red dome to ships putting in to English Bay, Vancouver, B.C. (Photo Leonard Frank Collection, Vancouver, B.C.)

STEAM REPLACED WATERPOWER when Croft and Angus converted the old Anderson mill in 1886. Three years later it was taken over by Victoria Lumber and Manufacturing Co., Ltd. Later H. R. MacMillan gained his first sawmill experience as salesman and assistant general manager of this company.

Anderson mill reached peak production in 1863 with one million board feet and closed in 1866 "for lack of wood in the district," a situation understandable considering the crude logging methods of the time. The first manager after Edward Stamp was Gilbert M. Sproat. (Photo from MacMillan and Bloedel Limited Collection)

THOMAS ASKEW'S DREAM CAME TRUE

In 1856 a group of settlers boarded a charted vessel at Fort Victoria and sailed north to Horse Shoe Bay on the east coast of Vancouver Island. There they landed and set about the business of making themselves secure. Most of them shunned the dense forest of the hinterland and preferred to hug the shoreline. Between themselves and the safety of Fort Victoria lay more than fifty miles of unbroken forest, forbidding indeed to those accustomed to sparse growth of the British Isles.

It might have been argued that the sea offered more menace to the newcomers than the forest. From the north, in long war-canoes came the dreaded Haidas who only a few years before the settlers' arrival had systematically wiped out the local Indians on the shoreline. Fortunately for the settlers the Haidas from that time onward seemed to make the journey southward for the sole purpose of buying "firewater" and supplies at Fort Victoria.

Some of the settlers chose to move inland and cleared land that has now developed into prosperous farms. Others lost their appetite for homesteading and drifted away. One of those who didn't seem to be interested in farming, but remained because he saw possibilities in other things, was Thomas George Askew. This man of great resource and vision saw possibilities in almost everything.

Askew, described by Governor Arthur Kennedy as "a hard-working and enterprising man, who landed here with half a dollar in his pocket," was the proud owner of a sawmill built in 1862. This mill, run by waterpower with an over-shot wheel, cost the owner, according to his own reckoning, $3,000.00, and produced between 1,500 and 2,000 feet of lumber in 11½ hours, the length of a working day in the 'sixties. This pioneer lumberman dreamed, he said, of this area becoming "one of the greatest lumber-producing centres on this coast."

CHEMAINUS MILL ON THIS SITE H.M.S. Firefly anchored off shore from Thomas Askew's house on Vancouver Island in 1873, was subject for this painting. Pioneer Askew built the first sawmill here, powered by water. He died in 1880. His widow operating mill until it was sold to Croft and Severne. (Photo from MacMillan and Bloedel Limited Collection)

Before long Askew, in his efforts to expand, ran afoul of his neighbors. Having been granted permission by Governor Kennedy to augment the water supply by diverting the overflow from Loon Lake (Chemainus) to Mill Stream, Askew began this project by building a dam at the lake outlet and digging a ditch to divert Askew Creek into Mill Stream.

On the trail Askew slashed through the woods to the lake was the farm of a settler named Clark Lambkin. Lambkin, however, belied his mild name by violently blocking Askew's attempts to reach the lake.

Askew wrote to the Surveyor General, "I went up to the Lake several time to try to find out who it was that was continually braking the dam and, as I was returning one evening in May last (1870) Lamkin came

out of his House and said he would shoot a valuable dog I then had with me, if I came that way again; and abused me in the most blackguardly manner."

Probably acting on the theory that "a man who would shoot a dog would shoot anything," Askew desisted. He again complained to the Surveyor General, "At present Lambkin or anyone else can Brake my Dam, and I shall not be able to get to it, or to take any Material for its Repair without being continually annoyed by one of the Worst and Meanest men in the Country." Continuing in the same vein, Askew declared that he had sold the property to Lambkin with the provision that a perpetual right of way be granted for the purpose of attending to the dam. In 1864, Askew asserted, he had bought this land "from a Mr. Guillod who then owned one-third share in the mill."

From this last line naturally arises the question of who was Mr. Guillod? Did Askew at that time own the other two-thirds, or were there two other co-builders? Unfortunately, the records of this period are sketchy and the question remains unanswered.

The colonial government of that time appears to have listened to Askew's arguments, at least in part, and to have deterred Lambkin from his blockade, with the provision that Askew avoid the Lambkin homestead. In requesting that the trail be made a public road, Askew wrote, "There is a large quantity of good land to the west of the Lake, that may at any day be settled, and this will be the most direct road to it."

The Surveyor General, seeing a chance to develop a public road out of a private quarrel, laid down his conditions. If Askew wanted a public road, all he had to do was to brush out the road, avoiding the fenced portion of the Lambkin place, grade the surface, do likewise to the Nanaimo Trail from the millsite to the Lake Road, and build a bridge over Askew Creek on this portion of the Nanaimo Trail. This "trifling" work completed, he said, the road would be declared a public right of way.

THOMAS ASKEW'S DREAM CAME TRUE After fire and financial crises, Chemainus mill of Victoria Lumber and Manufacturing Co. caught prosperity. Now subsidiary of H. R. MacMillan Export Company, Limited. (Photo B.C. Forest Service)

PAST THIS DOOR WALKED GREAT AND SMALL In 1892 a Chinese carpenter h a n d fashioned this heavy cedar door and fitted it with brass latch, toe plate and mail slot. For 59 years it was the main office door of the Chemainus, B.C., mill and swung back and forth for such visitors as Andrew Carnegie, John D Rockefeller on down to Brother Twelve a n d Princess ZEE, cult leaders who c a m e to buy lumber for their temple accompanied by pistol-packing henchmen. (Photo from MacMillan and Bloedel Limited Collection)

The project, when completed, was the first inland road in this district. Now known as Chapman Road, (North Chemainus) it cost the colonial government $22.50, the sum paid to Askew in compensation for his labour on the bridge. Complaining bitterly, Askew wrote, "The Bridge is 90 feet long and is worth $150 to the Government. I received $22.50 for my work on it."

With the source of the necessary water secure, Askew continued to operate his mill until his death in 1880. The discoverer of coal in the Ladysmith area in 1868, he left his name on many landmarks in the district.

It appears that Askew was the first to use the name Chemainus in referring to the settlement at Horse Shoe Bay. The present name is Askew's own way of spelling the Indian name of Tsiminnis, a legendary figure who led the migration of a tribe from the Alberni area to the head of Horse Shoe Bay.

Largely due to illness Askew did not see the fulfillment of his dream of Chemainus becoming "one of the greatest lumber-producing centres on the coast."

Mrs. Askew, after her husband's death, continued to operate the mill, but sold out to the firm of Croft and Severne in 1885. The new owners sent to England for a threshing machine engine and abandoned the waterwheel. With this steam power plant and additional machinery the mill grew in capacity and importance. In that same year construction of the E. & N. Railway commenced, bringing more orders for ties and lumber, more settlers, and consequently more demand for lumber.

Mr. Severne sold his interest and the firm became Croft and Angus. This new management improved and expanded their operation to meet the growing demands of the time. More machinery was installed and more men were required to operate the machines. Settlers cleared land in the surrounding district and sold their produce to the mill community and the camps. The new railway crawled along the coast of the Island and the Nanaimo Trail became the E. & N. right of way.

The year of 1887 saw the first train operating on the new railway. There was, however, no sawmill spur. Lumber for shipment by rail had to be hauled up the hill on wagons and stone-boats and loaded on the station siding.

The following year, Croft and Angus negotiated a sale to the Victoria Lumber & Mfg. Co. Ltd., which concern took over in 1889. The Croft & Angus mill was used to cut lumber for the construction of a new mill which started cutting in 1890. The new mill, however, was not complete at that time, and shut down for additions and improvements until finally completed in 1896.

There was little change in either mill or community until 1923. On November of that year disaster struck Chemainus. The mill caught fire, and in a matter of minutes was a mass of flames. The power house crew tied down the whistle cord before escaping, and above the roar of the flames the drone of the whistle went on until the mill foundation collapsed. Crowds of people lined the steep bank overlooking the millsite and watched their livelihood disappear in flames. Women wept and wrung their hands, then stood in the November dusk, staring at the red ashes. The people of Chemainus went home then and looked at one another, wondering — what now? Christmas of 1934 was bleak.

The new year brought hope to the community. The mill was to be rebuilt, and on a much larger scale. Soon fact caught up with rumour as landmarks disappeared and brush was cleared away to make room for the concrete foundations of the new plant.

In October, 1925, the new mill started production. Construction workers who came to build the mill stayed to work in it. More homes were needed and the face of Chemainus changed again as new homes arose where before only bush ringed the old town. Chemainus prospered until the depression throttled the lumber industry.

While the whole continent slowly emerged from the depths of the 1929 Depression, Chemainus began to spread out. One at a time, new homes cropped up on the outskirts of the town. The beginning of the World War temporarily stopped this trend, but with the end of hostilities came a boom in building both on the outskirts and near the millsite. New businesses moved in and new stores blossomed. The Victoria Lumber Company, reorganized in 1944 to become a subsidiary of H. R. MacMillan Export Co. Ltd., sponsored extensive housing projects and greatly improved plant facilities. Chemainus boomed, and is still booming. The dream of Thomas George Askew is now a reality. Here is "one of the greatest lumber-producing centres on the coast." — W. H. Olsen in H. R. MacMillan Export Company's "Harmac News."

McLAREN MILL GROWS UP

The barque *Mira* was readying for sea with 600,000 feet of lumber aboard. Her destination: Sydney, Australia.

It was mid-June, 1891, and the barque had arrived in tow of the tug *Active* at a site on the Fraser River, the village known as Millside which was destined to become Fraser Mills, one of the world's largest lumber shipping and wood processing points.

The original operation — the McLaren Mill — was built to cater to the export business. Its management is credited with playing a major role in the efforts to get the Fraser River dredged and open up nearby New Westminster as a deep-sea port.

In 1902, Lloyd's of London blacklisted the Fraser for deep ocean-going shipping, but by 1906, a permanent river pilot was guiding ships of 27-foot draft upstream to the sawmill's wharf to load for South Africa, Australia and the United Kingdom.

FIRST B.C. MILL TO EXPORT The Anderson Mill at Port Alberni was built in 1860 by Capt. Edward Stamp, land acquired from Indians for $100 worth of blankets and guns. They became annoying and threatened to stop construction work but pioneer William Banfield who spoke the native language, smoothed things out, laying down a strict code of conduct for white workers — no intoxicants, no fraternizing with the Indians, no indiscreet use of firearms.

MILL "IMPORTED" FRENCH-CANADIANS during 1909 labor shortage. This was Fraser Mills, originally the McLaren Mill at Millside on Fraser River, B.C., great export factor. Canadian Western Lumber Co. took over in 1910, then affiliated with Crown Zellerbach Canada, Limited. (Photo B.C. Provincial Archives)

In the years 1905-06-07-08, the McLaren mill was rebuilt and enlarged under the name of Fraser River Sawmills. In 1906, the Canadian Pacific Railway ran a special commuter's train over the four miles between New Westminster and the mill.

In 1909, a shortage of skilled sawmill workers resulted in the company arranging to bring out French-Canadian mill men from Quebec. A special C.P.R. 13-car train arrived from Montreal in October of that year with 110 workmen and their families. This migration resulted in the start of the French-speaking community of Maillardville, adjacent to the millsite.

By this time the sawmill was being advertised as the "largest and most up-to-date in Canada" and a branch line of the B.C. Electric Railway Company was built from New Westminster to the settlement, which had just been renamed Fraser Mills. At the same time, Fraser River sawmills was re-organized under a name which was to become synonymous with B.C.'s best lumber products — Canadian Western Lumber Company Limited.

Capitalization was increased and timber limits were purchased, mainly on Vancouver Island. During the next three years, the sawmill was modernized, a door factory and more employees' homes built and the market expanded to include the prairie provinces through purchase of retail outlets in Alberta and Saskatchewan. A plywood plant, completed in 1913, was the first Douglas fir plywood plant in Canada.

The company credits Henry J. Mackin for bringing the Canadian Western organization through difficult years. Mackin started as sales manager with the old Fraser River Sawmills in 1908, later became mill manager, then vice-president, director and general manager in 1936, and president and chairman of the Board in 1938. With the exchange of shares in 1953, Canadian Western became an affiliate of Crown Zellerbach Canada Limited.

ALBERNI'S FAMED FIVE

Initiative, ability and finances were pooled by four brothers to build what is now Alberni Pacific Lumber Division. Robert, Alexander, Norman and James Wood formed a corporation in November, 1904, and named it Barclay Sound Cedar Company. They took in Samuel Roseborough as a fifth partner, rolled up their sleeves and began to work.

Land for the proposed mill was bought south of the present commercial centre from the Anderson Land Company. Lumber to construct their living quarters on the mill site was bought from George Bird's little sawmill at the corner of Argyle and Bird streets. The cottage later became the Barclay Sound Cedar Company's office building.

Next came the need for machinery to cut lumber for mill construction. This they fulfilled by buying it from Joe Halpenny's mill at Rogers Creek, on the site of the present Tidebrook Hotel. To get the newly bought equipment to their own mill, Alex and nephew Roland Wood took a scow up the Somass River, poled, pushed and pulled it up Roger's Creek to Joe's mill. After loading the scow and taking advantage of tides they delivered it successfully to their millsite. This equipment incidentally, was reportedly the first machinery in British Columbia to cut lumber for export.

With this equipment the partners produced lumber for construction of the mill and sold their excess production to local residents. For the mill itself new machines were bought from the Robert Hamilton Agency, largely because Robert Wood was a good friend of Hamilton and had installed a lot of Hamilton's machines throughout British Columbia.

Daily production of lumber and shingles began in 1905 with a crew of ten men. Robert was manager, Alex, millwright; Norman, sawyer; George Bird, engi-

BEGAN AS BARCLAY SOUND CEDAR COMPANY owned by four Woods brothers and Samuel Roseborough. Through several ownership changes it became, in 1936, Alberni Pacific Lumber Co. Division of H. R. MacMillan Export Company, Limited. (Photo B.C. Forest Service)

neer; Fred Brand, engineer; nephew Roland Wood, general helper; Sam, a Chinaman, was fireman, and there was a Harry Truman, kin to Jack and Clayton Hills of Alberni (but no relation to the U.S. President!) The ten turned out 25,000 board feet of lumber per day . . . enough for two average-sized homes. James Wood looked after the office end of the company.

Several months previous to the mill's construction Robert and son Roland cruised timber and staked limits on Barclay Sound near the entrance to Alberni Inlet. They possessed limits around Silver Lake, across the inlet from the present Kildonan Cannery — then known as Charles Turnan's Cannery. They also owned a berth at San Mateo Bay.

The fifth partner of the company, Sam Roseborough, was logging foreman and also in charge of logging cedar shingle bolts at Useless Inlet. Camp buildings were on Vancouver Island proper but logging was conducted across the inlet on Sedall Island. These shingle bolts were cut mostly by local Indians. Three of the shingle makers, Billy Ucume, Tommy Bill and Frank Williams, are presently living on the reserve at Alberni.

The major logging area of the Barclay Sound Cedar Company was in and around the townsite of Port Alberni. A skid road was built east of the mill in the Bruce Street area and Douglas fir logs were hauled from there, and from the present hospital site, to the mill by teams of company-owned horses. Fred Brand logged the hospital area and dumped the logs into the inlet in the vicinity of the present Bloedel, Stewart and Welch pulp mill.

Fred left the Barclay Sound Company shortly after

the mill began operating in 1905 and went to Alaska as a steam engineer. Two years later, however, he returned to the company to become a donkey engineer at the Useless Inlet operation.

Log towing from dump to mill was handled by a chartered boat owned by an Irishman known as Black Mike. His boat was, appropriately enough, named "Shamrock." Later, however, the company bought their own tug, the "Troubador." Some time later the Troubador was working near Hell's Gate in the Alberni Inlet. It sank with Norman Wood aboard. Fortunately he managed to swim ashore and the tug was raised and sold.

Shipping their products to customers was a difficult proposition. Freighters had no regular run up the Alberni Inlet because insurance companies wouldn't give coverage to ships that had to round hazardous Cape Beale. Therefore the company had to charter ships to take their lumber to customers outside Alberni Valley. The first water shipment was cedar factory stock, dressed four sides. It is believed it was shipped on the "Otter Number Two" to Vancouver. Other sales were to West coast communities, Victoria and Vancouver.

In 1908, after three fairly prosperous years of operation, the Barclay Sound Cedar Company sold part interest to Carlin, Meredith and Gibson. Mike Carlin invested $125,000 in the concern. In the same year Mike brought in Joseph Hanna as manager, a position Joe held until the company was sold in 1912. At the time Joe Hanna became manager Walter Harris was clearing the townsite and leaving the logs where they fell. Joe's son Roy took

GREAT CENTRAL SAW-MILLS of B.C. Industries. (Photo B.C. Provincial Archives)

a contract to provide piles for the foundations of the first dry kiln. Roy hired a team of horses from Sam Roseborough for ten dollars a day. Two days later the company quit buying pilings . . . Roy was making too much money, a handsome net of $142.00 for two days work!

In 1909 the Wood brothers sold their interest in the mill to the firm of Meredith and Gibson. In 1912 the latter company bonded the mill, and a mill in Port Moody, with an English company for $1,225,000. The original Barclay Sound mill was then rebuilt, new machinery added and production upped to 125,000 board feet per day. It was renamed the Canadian Pacific Lumber Company. A year later, however, the mill went into

receivership and was taken over by the Dominion Bank.

In 1915 H. A. Dent leased the mill. A year later he began operations under a new name: Alberni Pacific Lumber Company. He continued to own and operate the mill until 1925, the year he sold the firm to Denny, Mott and Dickson, an English lumber company.

In 1936 the mill changed hands again. H. R. Mac-Millan Export Company bought it and has continued to operate it from that time on. In 1950 its name was changed slightly from "Company" to "Division" of the parent company of H. R. MacMillan Export Company Limited. . . . Mary Wood in H. R. MacMillan Export Company's "Harmac News.'

DARRINGTON MODERN Three Rivers Plywood and Timber Co. owned by E. E. and Roger A. Boyd, manufacturing on the scene made historic in highball logging days. (Photo courtesy E. E. Boyd)

HISTORIC WESTPORT

While now one needs only money — and plenty of it — to acquire a sawmill, in 1850 money alone was not important, and the first mill at Westport, Ore., was begun on a capital of seven dollars, American money.

John West, founder of Westport, lived in Quebec at the time gold was discovered in California. He rushed to the gold fields with the others, but when he got there he found that he was not a miner, and early in 1850 he left and came to Oregon on the steamship *Gold-Hunter*

To own a sawmill had been one of his greatest ambitions, so he began the search for a proper site. He knew what he needed — timber, power and transportation — and he spent all the spring of 1850 in a survey of the Willamette valley and the lower Columbia. Seventy-five miles below Portland, a little creek empties into a deep slough of the Columbia, and a short distance up the creek was a fair-sized water-fall. West discovered this in June. The banks of the slough were marshy and the brush was so thick that he had to chop his way to the fall. But he found all that he desired.

He had spent nearly all his money during his long search, but he began work on his mill immediately, in spite of the fact that he had only seven dollars. He cleared the site near the fall, built a skid-road, felled trees and whip-sawed boards. He made a crude water-wheel, and forged nearly all the ironwork himself. While he worked at his own mill, he added to his money capital by building a mill for George Abernathy at Prescott, Ore.

By June of 1856, he had completed both mills and began sawing lumber in his own. He worked from six in the morning to six at night, with an hour off at noon. He cut about twelve to fifteen hundred feet a day and for many years got a hundred dollars a thousand for his lumber. A lumber buyer in San Francisco said later that the timber in this locality was the finest yellow fir on the coast. As soon as he had his mill established, West built a store. Ships came twice a year from San Francisco with supplies for his and other stores and took return cargoes of lumber.

The logs cut up West creek were skidded down the road that he had built, with oxen; those cut on Plympton creek were floated to the mill through a flume West had built from one creek to the other. From the mill to the bank of the slough was built a tramway with four-by-four's for rails on which oxen pulled trucks or cars loaded with lumber to be shipped.

When West finished building his mill, he sent for his family, still in Quebec. They left in June, 1856, crossed the Isthmus of Panama, and finally arrived in Westport early in 1857. West had cleared some land for farming and built a log house, chinked with moss, to which his wife and daughters came, straight from the civilization of old Quebec. They were unused to hardships or isolation; they were lonesome, homesick, and afraid. The friendly and curious Indians frightened them by pushing the moss out of the cracks between the logs of their house to peer in at the strange white women.

The first lumber West cut in the mill was used to

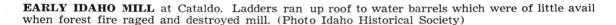

EARLY IDAHO MILL at Cataldo. Ladders ran up roof to water barrels which were of little avail when forest fire raged and destroyed mill. (Photo Idaho Historical Society)

GEORGE LITTLE'S SAW·MILL at Terrace, B.C., on Grand Trunk Pacific a n d Skeena River, 75 miles east of Prince Rupert. (Photo B.C. Forest Service)

build a house for his family. This was a comfortable and attractive dwelling of four rooms, built so sturdily that it is still in excellent condition. The sills, beams, joists, and other heavy timbers were fastened together with wooden pegs, driven through holes bored in them. then little wedges were driven into splits in the ends of the pegs. Anyone who has ever tried to wreck an old house built in this fashion knows how difficult it is to get the framework apart. The roof was of shakes. The floors are wide thick boards, still good, although in need of planing, as the house is built close to the ground, and having stood empty for some time, has drawn dampness, which caused the boards to buckle slightly. The stairway walls are of random width boards, none less than eight inches wide. The door and window trim is perfectly plain, rather narrow, with square corners, not rounded as is modern trim, and the windows are the double hung. six-light sash usually found in houses built at that time. The doors are particularly interesting. They are made in the inverted cross design, without ornamentation. heavy, and as good as new, although they have been in use for 75 years. They still have the old-fashioned thumb latches with which they were originally equipped. West made the doors and windows himself out of the native yellow fir.

The house, of good, straightforward design, is similar to those found in the New England states. Additions have been made to the original structure until now the house is completely modern.

West ran the water mill until early in the sixties. By then, the Pacific Coast was developing so rapidly and the demand for lumber was so insistent that the little mill was inadequate, and plans were made for a steam mill. West turned his interest over to his son David, who, with his cousin, John West, II, Frank Lovell, and Robert Thompkins, formed a new company and built the steam mill. This was fairly large for that time, being 126 feet long by 49 feet wide, and two stories in height. Nearly all the logs were brought from logging camps within two

or three miles of Westport, camps run by Sprague-Marsh, Crawford, Morgan, and others.

In 1868 the pioneer lumbermen shipped their first foreign cargo. The British ship *"Onward"* under Captain Whyte took a shipload of lumber for Melbourne and Sydney, Australia. After that, they shipped lumber all over the world and foreign orders still take a large share of the present company's cut.

In 1890 a logging camp, called Hungry Hollow, was built at the site of the old mill. A fine logging road was built up West creek for many miles. Where the creek had washed a deep canyon with sheer rocky walls, the road engineers built a log bridge. They hauled huge logs and dumped them into the bottom of the canyon. lengthwise, eight or ten feet apart. On these they piled others, crosswise, and so on to the top, which they covered entirely with small logs, in the customary corduroy effect.

The same ingenious engineers who built the bridge also dug a tunnel under the point of the hill which jutted out in their way. The logging road ran through the tunnel, and the logs were hauled down, through the tunnel. and dumped into a ditch, to be floated down to the slough and down that to the pond. About 35,000 feet were brought down at each load, which required 14 oxen to pull it. The men all worked 12 hours a day, the skidders usually longer.

The skid road was greased to make the logs slide easily, so barrels of grease were placed at convenient intervals. It was necessary for the logging company to employ a brave night watchman whose sole duty was to guard this grease from the all too numerous bears, as they considered skid grease more delicious than honey.

In time the old Westport Lumber Co. sold the plant to Robert Suitor. He in turn sold it to Blinn and Waldo, from whom it passed to Palmer and Stoddard, and from them to The Westport Lumber Co.. the present owners. —Charlotte K. Geisler in 4 L Lumber News March 1, 1932.

MILLS *for the* RAIL TRADE

Up to 1900 most Washington sawmills were small ones cutting for local homes and industry and the large ones shipping by water to California and foreign ports. Then came the railroads with freight rates to Minneapolis of 40 cents a hundred. Timber owned by the railroads was sold to the big sawmill interests which suddenly got bigger.

One was St. Paul and Tacoma Lumber Co. with C. W. Griggs at its head. This firm bought 80 thousand acres from the Great Northern Railway and began cutting 500 thousand feet of lumber and 400 thousand shingles a day. At this time the Port Blakely mill was the largest in the world under one roof. The Larson Lumber Company in Whatcom County was booming as was the Grays Harbor Commercial Company, a Pope and Talbot subsidiary, Tacoma Mill Co. and Stetson-Post Lumber Company in Seattle. A decade later Clear Lake Lumber Company, just south of Sedro-Woolley, challenged all big Puget Sound mills in production.

In 1901, when logs were selling at $4 a thousand,

$30,000 built a big sawmill on Washington's Lake Whatcom. This was the mill of the Larson Lumber Company, the first Bloedel-Donovan enterprise, of which wealthy builder of railroads Peter Larson was president. The Hastings Shingle Mill, a few miles north, was purchased. Then C. L. Flynn was made general superintendent, John McMahon hired to run the existing sawmill, and in 1907 a new mill was built at another location on the lake.

Ten years after their first band wheel turned, Bloedel-Donovan Lumber Mills had become one of the largest all-rail shippers of the Pacific Northwest, producing 75 million feet of lumber and 150 million shingles a year. In 1911 sales headquarters were in Seattle and a retail subsidiary was organized — Columbia Valley Lumber Co. with yards covering Eastern Washington. In 1920 the company bought timber in Clallam County and on both sides of the Nooksack River and with the entrance of railroad contractors Stewart and Welch, became one of the powerful latter day lumber factors of Puget Sound.

LEUDINGHOUSE BROTHERS in Doty-Dryad area tapped the fine timber along the Northern Pacific line from Chehalis to South Bend. (Photo courtesy H. B. Onn)

PRIDE OF DOTY was this combination m i l l of Doty Lumber a n d Shingle Co. (Photo courtesy H. B. Onn)

THE NIGHT SHIFT

by JAMES STEVENS

From early youth James F. Stevens ate the dust of labor in many fields and on this firm footing became a novelist with "Brawnyman" and chronicler of the Paul Bunyan legends. His subsequent writings and activities have always started from the premise that the physical struggle of man is necessary to his full affirmation of life. When "The Night Shift" was written his feelings toward sawmills and sawmill people were earnest and now they live again.

By day a sawmill is a sprawling, ugly, greasy, dusty place of labor. The screams of the saws, the roar of machines, the booming of lumber along the rolls are exactly those sounds, and no more. In the harsh light of day illusions haven't a chance. But at night there is a change. Take a rainy winter night, just before the starting whistle sounds, when twilight is fading into deep darkness. Then a certain romance and color moves over the sawmill scene. The arc lamps over the piles and trams glow softly through slanting lines of rain. The burner is no longer a black towering bulk, but its ruddy dome seems to burn into the lowering sky, and brilliant swarms of sparks fly out from it in the night wind. The mill house is shadowy except for the yellow squares of light which mark its windows. There is a white glare over the markers' table and along the green chain. Up in the lights and shadows of the mill itself the screams of the saws are transformed into songs. The headsaw, streaming with water, glitters in a dazzle of light. It is a cheerful scene of labor, and the atmosphere is inspiring. Even the square-jawed mill boss seems to wear a kinder expression at night. One no longer notices the tobacco juice on his chin, and his commands, for all their profanity, are spoken in a tender tone.

Any man who has worked the night shift never forgets the lure of the lights. Getting a day job, he may realize that it is better for his health, that it gives him more leisure in hours when movies are shown and dances put on and stud poker played, but he misses something in his work. It seems cold and drab. Other day-shifters appear to have no fraternal spirit. The boss-men are all for business. Life is an eternal monotony of rising at 6, grouching through a breakfast, plugging away to work, putting in the hours, and resting along until bedtime. Before

CHEHALIS RIVER VALLEY yielded fine fir and cedar for years but many of its towns are ghosts today. McCormick Lumber Co. at McCormick had rough going in the latter days but was booming when Darius Kinsey took this picture in 1915. (Darius Kinsey photo from Jesse E. Ebert)

long the day-shifter is fishing around, trying to snare a night job again.

That has happened several times to me, and I have seen it happen to many others. When I worked in the sawmills of the Northwest coast I was a confirmed night-shifter. East of the mountains, where shifts were changed every two weeks, I often tried to start a Western Oregon revolt against the pine country custom, but never succeeded. Shift-changing, I still maintain, is a bad policy for any sawmill. The best sawyers and lumber-handlers naturally take to night-shift work — as I did. Where shift-changing is in effect these superior men are hampered in their efforts to make lumber manufacture profitable by being mixed with inferior day-shifters and bound down by two weeks of day work each month. In the Douglas fir mills, where shift-changing is not practiced, the men on the night shifts make such large profits for their employers that they can afford the luxury of supporting day-shifters. The pine manufacturers should also give the best sawyers and lumber-handlers the opportunity of grouping together and working the hours most natural to them.

The reason for this general superiority of the night-shifter over the day man lies in his superior intelligence. A heady man will, on the average, perform a given job better than a dumb man. And in sawmill work the heady men naturally take to the night shift. Its advantages are soon obvious to the sawmill-worker of intelligence.

Consider, for example, the important question of saving money. The night-shifter has a great advantage here. He is not tempted to ramble to a movie every evening, for one thing. For another, it is difficult for a radio

salesman to coax him into buying a set, for he is always at work when the good programs are on the air. Neither do dances, bridge parties and poker sessions trouble him much, for these amusements flourish mostly at night. Consequently, he misses most of the temptations to waste his savings. If the day-worker replies that a man should have enough will power to resist such temptations anyway, the night-shifter has this comeback: "Well, why haven't *you* got the will power?"

In his relations with the fair sex the night-shifter also has much the best of it. If he is single and is enamored of one of the hotel waitresses he does his courting at an hour when it cannot cost him much money. The young lady has perhaps an hour off in the afternoon, and an hour a day is enough for any clever, good-looking night-shift lad. He knows for certain whether she is kidding him along for the sake of a paying escort to movies, dances and restaurant feeds. He can't escort her in the afternoon, so he knows that when she welcomes his attentions the welcome is from her heart. The married night-shifter also has his benefits. The kids are at school or out playing during his hours of rest. Neither he nor his wife is weary from a long day of work. He feels fresh and kind from a good rest. He has no quarrels with his wife. The children regard him as an affectionate father, and not as a crank who makes them keep quiet as mice through a long evening. The intelligent married man always prefers the night shift.

The young man who wants to get ahead in the lumber business prefers the night shift as a matter of course. Working days, he would be too weary from his labors to study grading and other paperwork effectively at

FAMOUS LITTLE PRESTON MILL of Preston Lumber Co. west of Seattle. (Photo courtesy Mrs. A. E. Coppers)

night. Working nights, he is refreshed and rested from a good sleep when he has the leisure to take to his books. What he has studied is still clear in his mind when he goes to work and he practically applies it. In every Douglas fir mill where I worked in my lumbering days I found that the serious and studious hands were invariably on the night shift, while the giddy-minded young jazz hounds would only work days. Such conditions plainly indicate that the high-powered executives of the future in the lumber industry will all be men who spent their youth working night shift.

The labor itself in a sawmill night shift is infinitely more agreeable than it is in the daytime. There are even purely mechanical advantages, for — in my opinion — it is easier to grade logs and lumber by powerful artificial light than by natural daylight. Certainly the grading is always done better on the night shift, though this fact, again, may be accounted for by the night-shifters' usually superior intelligence. But the chief charm of night work is in the atmosphere it creates. Under the clusters of lights in the mill and along the green chain is a world of its own. The rest of life is shut out by darkness. Here is a family, one feels, in which all are kind-hearted brothers. The bitter rivalries of the day men are seldom repeated in the night shift. All feel bound together, and they work together in harmony, while on the day shift the individualistic spirit prevails and it is every man for himself. That is because the man working in the cold

light of day sees only a plain job under his hands. To him the sawmill and the yards are only a feature in a wide general landscape.

I recall in particular the difference between the day view and the night view from the station I worked on the green chain of the sawmill at Westport. The day man looked out on a drab scene — shop buildings, slab piles, and an open waste pile which was only an ugly, black, smoking mass in the daytime. Certainly there was everything depressing in the spectacle. And, of course, the day man on that station was a thick-skulled Greek. (He was, by the way, the vilest load-builder that ever wore an apron.) At night, however, that station opened on a scene of beauty. Against the lights of the millhouse windows the shop buildings were shadowy bulks, and the slab piles might have been the walls of ancient cities. The waste pile was no longer ugly and black. Flames lifted from it in fiery figures against the darkness. Sparks swarmed out from it in the wind. From its sides smoldering coals stared out like red eyes. The whole scene was a feast for the imagination and I never ceased to enjoy it.

There was a particular strong sense of comradeship among the men of the night shift. The day men had their own individual interests and perhaps got together only for occasional poker sessions or for a 4L meeting in the evenings. But the night-shifters all ganged around in the hotel lobby when the 4 o'clock lunch was finished. A half an hour was needed to talk over the various events

NO BURNER AT SEATTLE-RENTON MILL Sawdust at this long-operating mill was sold locally for fuel. (Darius Kinsey photo from Jesse E. Ebert)

of the shift just ended and to get them off our minds. Then the spirit of the old days of lumbering blazed up again. Tremendous arguments were started. "Take a drive wheel of a locomotive traveling 30 miles an hour," one would say. "Does the top of the wheel go faster than the bottom?" It took three weeks, as I remember, to get rid of that particular argument; and even then certain stubborn adherents of the losing negative side were still to be seen rolling snoose boxes across the floor and staring at them, trying to discover in this way some means to prove that these other stiffs were crazy.

But the tall tales were the chief feature of the get-together hour after 3 o'clock in the morning. Bill Schwartz, then the edgerman, invariably started them. He had sawmilled in Alaska for years, and he had some astounding yarns about salmon mines, ice worms and the like. No one ever disputed them, of course, and no one ever surpassed them until a stray sagebrusher landed in our midst. His first session he left everybody gasping with a story of how he had settled a dispute over wages with the North Bank railroad by getting an attachment on all their rolling stock.

"Yep, I closed the whole railroad down solid for three hours," he said. "Not a wheel moved."

Later on he modestly admitted that he had once moved a ten-ton tractor three miles by himself. He simply twisted the flywheel around and around with his brawny arms. Nobody could bring up a subject but what he would top it with something that had happened East of the Mountains. His most monumental success was with a hunting story. Bill Schwartz had just ended quite a handsome tale about bear-killing in Alaska, when our sagebrusher horned in.

"You talk about huntin' with a high-powered rifle and killin' two grizzlies with one shot as though *that* was news," the sagebrusher sneered. "You'd tell that to a man East of the Mountains and you'd shore get the horse laff. You take me now. I don't claim to be much of a hunter; East of the Mountains I ain't considered much at all. But I did do fair with a double-barrel shotgun one time. I was down on a river bottom when I sighted some quail. Got excited and give 'em both barrels. The infernal shotgun blowed up. Well, sirs, when the smoke had cleared away I discovered that the shot had killed all the quail, the shattered bits of one barrel had flew upstream and killed six Chiny pheasants, the other barrel had busted downstream and killed as many grouse, one hammer had hit a coyote between the eyes and knocked him cold, the other had busted all the ribs of a badger, the kick of the shot had knocked me back on a rattlesnake so's I tromped him dead, the stock had sailed on and knocked over a rabbit, and as it went it had ripped off my coat and flung it over a cougar's head and smothered him. Purty fair killin,' you'll say. But not much East of the Mountains, where the real hunters are. No, sir."

Bill Schwartz had to be carried up to bed that night, and all of us went around with dazed looks for about a week. We were thankful when the sagebrusher departed for his home country and a sheep-herding job. He had almost wrecked our night shift, and it was too good a life to lose. There is no other like it for a sawmill man. May its lights never go out.

—4L Lumber News, November, 1928

A "COOKHOUSE SHOW" was the logging chance of White River Lumber Co. with timber right down to the pond, the mill taking only The Big Fir. Fire in 1902 wiped out mill but spared 3-mile flume to planing mill. (Photo courtesy Weyerhaeuser Timber Co. White River Branch)

THE WHITE RIVER STORY

"On June 20, 1902, the White River Lumber did not start its mill. The air was very heavy with smoke, the sky was dark and yellowish. On the following morning there was no mill to start. June 20 was the day of the disastrous fire which completely destroyed the little mill and all the camp buildings at Ellenson and came within an inch of making a clean sweep of the downtown planing mill and the town itself.

"The fire started in the morning. There had been fires around the country. The woods were dry and 1902 was to go down on record as one of the most disastrous years for forest fires in the Douglas Fir region of Western Washington and Oregon.

(opposite) **PENINSULA LUMBER COMPANY — PORTLAND** (Photo Oregon Collection, University of Oregon)

"Around the little mill three miles east of Enumclaw in June 1902 there were many snags; the ground was covered with brush. A dry, hot East wind swept down. Then suddenly the flames roared up to the East of the mill, swept toward the mill at a terrific pace and engulfed all, mill, camp, and timber. The people at the mill were helpless, so fast and furious came the flames. They could only save themselves, and this they did by running out on the cleared flat where the log pond is now. There were two or three little farms there at the time, and by some miraculous turn of events these farm buildings escaped destruction.

"People grabbed what personal belongings and furniture they could from the camp and threw them into the creek, seeking to save them from the fire. It is said that Robert Thim for a time was thought lost, but saved himself by following up the creek, and that Henry Thim went home and changed his shoes, putting on his new ones with the hope of saving them. Many people did unaccountable things in the heat of the excitement.

"For a time it seemed that the people at Ellenson would be trapped, for the fury of the flames evidently

69

WOMAN'S PLACE IN THE HOME? MULLARKY! Not in wartime when women had to take men's places. "Nothing soft about some of the women we had," says Jack McKinnon at White River. Most of them toughened up and did a good job. Typical at White River in 1943 was headsaw off-bearer Mrs. Viola Wilkening.

created a draft which resolved itself into a strong wind blowing toward the East up the creek to meet the flames. There was fire all around.

"The logs in the little mill pond burned flat to the water, but the sawdust which had been flumed down along the creek bottom from the sawmill and which lay there in a big pile was only scorched a little on the surface. The people at the camp took note of this after the fire, and when the second fire in September once again destroyed the camp buildings and all but took the mill then partially rebuilt — for a second time — the wise ones went out and buried their belongings in the sawdust for safekeeping.

"The flames of the June fire raced down to the very edge of Enumclaw and there all hands concentrated to save the planing mill. It was a tight squeak because the fire came right up to the edge of piles of lumber in the outdoor drying yard. The mill over in Buckley shut down and men came over to help fight the fire in their neighboring village.

"At the Enumclaw railroad depot a train stood ready to evacuate the town's population. Men flung themselves down exhausted. Everything was tinged with an eerie yellow from the dense smoke. Women made coffee and served it to the struggling men. Great burning brands flew over the city and villagers watched their roofs with anxious eyes. But the town itself was saved. Men who were in the thick of the battle for survival of the community itself were blind from the smoke for several days after.

"Arvid Tell can recall that the 1902 fire burned the wooden cab off the No. 1 logging locomotive. Tell made a trip to another company's camp to get the measurements on a cab so that he could build another for the 'One Spot.'

"After the fire had passed 'many of the people were pretty blue at first' — as some now describe it — with the disaster. They wondered about the future. The mill was gone. Would it rebuild again? There was not a cent of insurance. But with prompt determination the men

WHITE RIVER CAMP ABOUT 1900 Steam from wood-burning Climax plumes up behind shacks. Men walked to and from woods and mill, worked ten hours for $2 and $2.25. (Photo courtesy Weyerhaeuser Timber Co. White River Branch)

of White River Lumber Co. immediately set about to rebuild. They were in the lumber business to stay."

So reported the Enumclaw (Wash.) Courier-Herald on this phase in the 67 year struggle and strides of the White River Lumber Co. from the little 1890 mill of Charles Magnus Hanson and his sons at Eddyville to the 1933 alignment with Weyerhaeuser Timber Co.

The White River story actually started in 1896 when the four Hansons — father Charles and sons A. G., Charles S. and Frank — with Louis Olson and Alex Turnbull formed a company and took over the Goss sawmill at Ellenson and the burned-out planing mill at Enumclaw. Fred E. Robbins shortly bought out Turnbull's interest and in '98 operated the company's retail outlet in Ritzville.

Then came the 1902 holocaust. A. G. Hanson had gone East for machinery to rebuild the mill when a second fire all but destroyed it a second time that year. But with the installation of band mill and other new equipment, the plant was soon cutting 100 thousand feet

a day. During the next few years, mill, logging and rail improvements brought production up while safety precautions kept disaster out. But in 1906 came the death of Charles Magnus Hanson. Son Charles S. then became president, serving until his own death in 1919. During the first 40 years of White River's advance, A. G. Hanson was the dominating influence and is credited with the company's financial success. Lou Olson was president until the Weyerhaeuser merger. Louis Garfield "Gar" Olson, eldest son of Ellen Hansen, who had married Lou Olson, then became general manager of the White River Division.

The 3-mile lumber flume to the Enumclaw planing mill was fed by Boise Creek and always necessitated the sawmill starting a half-hour earlier to get boards "to town" by 7:30. It was used until the mill was rebuilt in 1931. This constituted a "logging operation." With the sawing floor of the old mill supported by a network of track ties it was skidded with woods equipment to the new mill location.

PLANER SPEED 70 FEET per minute in this 1903 planing mill of White River Lumber Co. — 3 miles by flume from sawmill. Planers used square arbors with two knives which mill itself ground. (Photo courtesy Weyerhaeuser Timber Co. White River Branch)

LADY GANGSTER At White River gangsaw is Mrs. Ada Moultrie who had 13 living children. (Photos of women by Kenneth S. Brown)

HEADSAW AND CARRIAGE AT SNOQUALMIE FALLS Lumber Co. a steady and important Weyerhaeuser producer and mainstay of economy in Snoqualmie Valley, Wash. Mill was built in 1916, managed by Warren, with Cutler Lewis as logging superintendent. (Darius Kinsey photo from Jesse E. Ebert Collection)

GOLD RUSH STARTED OLYMPIC AREA LUMBERING

"When the gold rush hit California in 1849 and mining camps sprang up overnight," said the Port Angeles News of Nov. 28, 1953, "lumber was urgently needed for building the boom towns. There were no harbors tapping the Northern California timber so California turned to Washington for Douglas fir.

"Ships from the East Coast converged on San Francisco and first sought hewn timbers to be carried to California for resawing. By the time Washington had become a territory early settlers were doing a thriving business in furnishing them. They cut and squared the timbers and schooner skippers bargained for them at water's edge.

"In 1852, a year before Washington became a territory, a sawmill was built at Port Ludlow. The Port Gamble mill started operations in 1853. The Discovery Bay mill started sawing lumber in 1858 and the Port

300,000,000 FEET A YEAR in lumber and shingles were cut in the big inland mill of Clear Lake Lumber Co. at Clear Lake, Washington. In 1920, its operations were expected to "last forever" yet today hardly a trace remains of the mill or timber workings. (Darius Kinsey photo from Jesse E. Ebert Collection)

Townsend mill in 1859. Soon afterwards the Hadlock mill on Port Townsend bay was in production.

"Other mills at Seattle and Port Blakely, further up Puget Sound, were operating about the time Washington Territory was created.

"By this time new cities were being built in the territory. The sawmills supplied the local demand, but the bulk of the lumber went to California on sailing vessels. Many of the schooners and square riggers, were built and owned by the big sawmill companies.

"The quality of the timber attracted a man from San Francisco to start a mill of his own. He was S. B. Mastick, who opened the Port Discovery Mill in 1858.

"Nearest mill to Clallam County was at Discovery Bay, just east of the Clallam-Jefferson County line. Clallam County touched on the northern end of the bay at Diamond Point, on the tip of the Blyn Peninsula. The Discovery Bay mill company cut much of the timber on Blyn Peninsula and west to Dungeness.

"The first mill in the Sequim area was operated by Chris Miller and later purchased by Fowler and Smith. William Long and associates bought it in 1902, moving it to the Dungeness River. R. W. Long and his son E. R. Long, owned the Port Williams mill which started operating in 1906. J. L. Keeler had a sawmill in the community

HALF MILLION MEALS A YEAR came out of this kitchen and on these tables for crews of Snoqualmie Falls Lumber Co. (Cress-Dale photo from University of Washington)

of Sequim and other small mills were owned by Ed Potter and Charles, George and Henry Fitzgerald.

"Shingle production in the Olympic area started in 1887 when the Puget Sound Cooperative Colony built its mill at Ennis Creek on Port Angeles harbor. That same year a shingle mill was built in the Dry Creek area and owned by L. T. Haynes, William Graham, Clarence McLaughlin, Nicholas Meagher Jr., Ray Haynes and Frank Patton. The shingles were hauled to the head of Port Angeles harbor and shipped on the steamer Evangel.

"A second mill was built in the Dry Creek district in 1889 by the Port Angeles Shingle and Lumber Co. The lumber and shingles were hauled to the head of the harbor over a tramway. Norman R. Smith constructed the mill for the company. When these mills ceased operations the Eacrett brothers, Richard and Will built a mill there that operated for years.

"By the 90's many shingle mills were being erected through the county. Usually they were near large stands of timber. In some instances the cedar logs were split into 'bolts' and hauled to the mills. In other places the logs were dumped into mill ponds.

"Some of the mills were combination shingle and lumber, but many were small mills cutting shingles exclusively. The Wait brothers, Miles and E. R., operated a shingle mill directly south of Port Angeles for many years.

"The late G. M. Lauridsen financed many of the mills. He handled the payrolls and marketed the products. It was during these years that Lauridsen issued his own scrip, which was good for trade in his store here.

"One of the most famous mill sites was near the present boat haven. The first shingle mill was built there in 1899. It operated under various ownerships. In 1917 a group of 25 employes took it over, and it was known as the Co-Op-Mills, as all who worked there held stock in the company. It was taken over by the M. R. Smith Co. in 1925, and that company moved the plant to Lake Pleasant in 1940.

"When the Puget Sound Mills and Timber Co. built the 'big mill' here in 1914 a shingle and lath manufacturing plant was incorporated with it. This was the first mill here to export lumber. The mill had its own dock, and its lumber and shingles went by ships and rail all over the world."

PAIR OF ACES Twin mills of McCloud River Lumber Co. at Weed, Calif. (Photo University of Washington)

SAWMILLS OF SOUTHWESTERN SISKIYOU

In the fifty-mile area southwest of Mt. Shasta probably sixty sawmills have operated since 1860. A few of them have historical importance beginning with the first mill in Siskiyou County. This was a waterpower mill at the head of the Shasta River southwest of Edgewood using a sash saw and built by the China Ditch Co. about 1853. It was bought in 1854 by J. A. Maxwell who with his six sons ran it until sold to Jim Dobkins in 1888 by which time it had been changed over to a circular mill.

Meanwhile a steam mill had been built three miles south of the present site of Weed by a Mr. Hearst and it was purchased in 1883 by one of the Maxwell sons, Milton P. Another son, J. H., joined him and Maxwell Brothers operated the mill until 1894 when it was bought by Abner Weed. Two years later he built a new mill at Weed and in 1903 incorporated the Weed Lumber Co. Three years later J. M. White started work there, then went to Long-Bell Lumber Co. becoming its president in 1916. That firm bought the controlling interest in the Weed mill and in 1926 it became Long-Bell's Weed Division.

The Ross McCloud mill at Soda Springs was built in 1859 and included a flume to bring water to the power wheel. In 1886 a timber claim was filed and the first mill built in the Shasta Springs area by James J. Scott, Joseph Schaefer, Walter Shattuck and Mark Neher. After the springs were sold to the Shasta Water Company, Scott moved the sawmill to Hedge Creek, it became the Scott and Rex mill and was sold to Leland, Wood and Sheldon in 1896.

That year this firm, Sisson Mill and Lumber Co. also bought the mill which later became known as the Big Mill, built in 1890 by Bernard, Wallbridge and Huntington, near the present site of Shasta Pine Manufacturing Co. in Sisson. In 1901 Leland sold out.

Wood and Sheldon purchased the small Loy box factory south of the Big Mill and moved it to the Sacramento River at the head of Box Canyon where it became known as the first Rainbow Mill. It was later moved to a point south of Deer Creek. One of the Wood and Sheldon partners, named Martin, organized the Pioneer

McCLOUD RIVER FORE-RUNNER 1898 sawmill of Scott and Van Arsdale Lumber Co. at Upton, Calif., built just after the Southern Pacific Railroad came up Sacramento River canyon. Mill was later moved up river to present site McCloud River Lumber Co. Note lumber used for tram car rails. (Photo Schroeder Collection Collier State Park Logging Museum)

Box Co. and took over the mill. In 1914 Wood and Sheldon liquidated. Frank Ball and William Giesendorfer, who had operated a mill at Truckee and managed the Truckee Lumber Co. mill at Cantara, organized the Rainbow Mill and Lumber Co. which took over the Sisson Mill and Lumber Co.

As the Southern Pacific Railroad pushed north from Redding, many small tie mills sprang up. One was Charles Wright's, two miles north of Sisson. In the early '90s, Scott and Van Arsdale purchased this, supplying fuel and ties to the Southern Pacific. They also started the town of Upton and built a narrow gauge railroad — the beginning of the McCloud River Railroad.

Farley and Letcher built a box factory south of Upton in 1896. Scott and Van Arsdale planned to erect a bigger plant on the railroad near Sisson where the Big Lakes Box Factory was later built. They imported sixty Chinese laborers and camped them. The local citizens were incensed, raided the camp and sent the Chinese packing. Scott and Van Arsdale rounded them up, placed a guard on the camp and at a town meeting told the people to let the Chinese alone, that they were doing dirty work

making a fill which white men wouldn't do. They warned that if the camp was molested, the mill would not be built. Two weeks later, the camp was raided again, some Chinamen kidnapped and loaded on a box car. All of them departed and so did Scott and Van Arsdale. They bought the sawmill of Friday George on the McCloud River, the company eventually progressing into the McCloud River Lumber Company. The town of Upton disappeared except for the big piles of sawdust.

In 1886 as the Southern Pacific pushed ahead to Mott above Shasta Springs, a waterpower mill was built above the Springs by John W. Davis, Fred Florin and William Powers — the Mott Manufacturing Co. Later Davis bought out his partners and started a mill at Small. In 1890 two other mills were built in this vicinity — the Red Cross Mill and David Miles Box Factory. About this time, Nelson and McKenzie built their second mill south of Sisson near the McCloud Station on the Southern Pacific, their first mill being on the north side of Big Canyon. (From article by George R. Schrader in Siskiyou County Historical Society Yearbook 1948)

OREGON MAMMOTH Huge plant of Pacific Spruce Lumber Co., Toledo, Oregon. (Photo Oregon Historical Society)

TIMBER *at* TIDEWATER

"Aberdeen better than San Francisco? There ain't much difference. The size maybe, right now. But that Aberdeen is more like to get places. Timber? You never saw the likes of it. Man, up there in Grays Harbor the cows eat sawdust!"

In 1910 the course of empire seemed to be west to the Pacific right through the greatest blanket of fir and cedar the United States ever knew. Grays Harbor looked like the place prosperity would pick to settle down in. Loggers and sawmill men were pushing north from California and Oregon. The word was going around Puget Sound that Aberdeen and Hoquiam were going to boom so get over there fast. Trains from Chicago and Minneapolis were bringing in thousands of workers and millions in working capital. This was going to be the Lumber Capitol of the World — the biggest lumbering and shipping area in the country's biggest lumbering state.

If a sawmill boomer had started out of Tacoma that year and worked out his bunk and beans for three days in every mill he walked up to, it would have taken him two years to complete a loop south of Olympia to Chehalis, west to South Bend and then to Aberdeen and Hoquiam via Elma and Montesano. And by that time fifty more sawmills would have sprung up and he would have had to start all over again and run fast past a hundred little shingle mills.

He was in lumber country right enough. Tacoma was rivalling Portland in production. About that time Pacific National, Gale Creek, Puget Sound, Eastman, Keystone, Capitol Box, Pacific Box, Tacoma Mill, Doud Brothers, Winkleman, St. Paul and Tacoma, Ernest Dolge, Clear Fir, Western Fir, Dempsey, Danaher and twenty more mills around Tacoma were ripping logs and crying for men. Olympia had Olympia Door, Olympia Manufacturing along with Keyes Shingle, National Pipe and Buchanan. In the hinterland were Lindstrom and Hanford, Mumby, Manley-Moore, Bordeaux and Fairfax.

When the boomer went south he would have hit Blumauer, Stone Brothers, Mentzer Brothers and Jones Spar in Tenino — H. J. Miller, Chehalis Fir and Coal Creek in Chehalis, Eastern Railway and Lumber and others in Centralia. Napavine would have turned up Central Lumber and George McCoy — Winlock, Emery and Veness, S. W. Porter and perhaps the shop where

HOQUIAM INSTITUTION Mill of Northwestern Lumber Co., a mainstay of Hoquiam industry for many years. (Photo University of Washington)

HOQUIAM ABOUT 1900 Sawmill at left cuts timber for ship being built at right. (Photo University of Washington)

Andrew Johnson shaped his famous ship knees.

In Littel he would have found Wise Lumber and in Doty and Dryad half a dozen mills as well as McCormick on west. Raymond was booming with Clarin and Hamilton, J. A. Heath, Willapa Harbor, Raymond Lumber, Kolb and Gilbert and Siler. South Bend had Kleeb and the Simpson Lumber which was shipping by rail and schooner.

Back up in Elma the short staker might have learned that Henry McCleary was building a big mill at Summit, that Vance Lumber was shut down for bigger and better things to come and White Star would be cutting 20 million feet of lumber and 50 million shingles this year. Montesano Lumber was working a hundred men. And then — Aberdeen.

The short-staker would now see that this was not only as far as he could go without drifting out to sea but that this was a country full of working stiffs — and he

(opposite) **SCHAFER BROTHERS MILLS.** Big time logging operators, Schafer Brothers started buying sawmills and shingle mills in 1919. Upper left, plant on Chehalis River, Aberdeen; lower right, Montesano shingle operation. **HOQUIAM SAWMILLS** in an early day. Upper right, E. K. Wood Lumber Co. of which George Kellogg was longtime manager; lower left, "Big Mill" of Hoquiam Lumber and Shingle Co. (Photos Frank Eno Collection)

would have to make up his mind what to do. He might ask around — what was going on? Logging, sawmilling, shipyards and everything that went with them. The bulls were out of the woods and steam donkeys had taken over. Skidroads were now railroads. Mills? The big ones were Anderson and Middleton, which had taken over the Weatherwax interests, the Old Folks Home across the river at Cosmopolis and the Northwest in Hoquiam. Plenty of others needing men though.

The Hart-Wood Lumber Co. was running ten hours and Western Lumber had just added to its capacity. In fact they were having a ship built by Lindstrom Ship Building Co. — the *Quinault* they were going to call it. The Lindstrom yard had built fifty vessels the year before, now just finishing two big rock barges for the Columbia River and three steam schooners for the Coast trade. John Lindstrom was mayor of Aberdeen and had just returned from San Francisco. "There's a piece in the paper about it," somebody said. Lindstrom says this town's got too fast a gait so he's going to clamp the lid on. Don't worry, son, it won't last more than two or three days. How you going to keep this hot town under cover. Let 'er buck!"

American Mill Co. was going great guns — Wilson

GRAYS HARBOR CITY NEVER GOT STARTED Plans to dike tidelands and create deepwater harbor on which sawmills would be built led to promotion of Grays Harbor City. Plans proved too advanced and project failed. (Photo Frank Eno Collection)

Brothers, too. Aberdeen Lumber and Shingle was turning out 5 million shingles and a quarter of a million feet of lumber a month and going to rail trade as well as ship cargo. Western Cooperage employed a hundred men now. A. J. West was building a new mill. Michigan Lumber had just finished one — a lath mill — and was enlarging the planing mill. It had just cut some 90-foot timbers and was going to make bevel siding. And what about S. E. Slade Lumber Co.? Running their own logging camps by railroad and cutting a monthly average of 6½ million feet.

Over in Hoquiam, E. K. Wood was bearing down on production and had just launched the ship *Tamopais* to keep up its export business. Northwestern Lumber Co., the first mill here, was making things hum, and so was the Hoquiam Sash and Door and Hoquiam Lumber and Shingle Co. This was the new name of Robert F. Lytle's mill. With his brother Joseph, he had logged here since 1889, building his shingle mill in 1905. National Lumber and Box operated a big mill and Grays Harbor Lumber Co. was a big rail and water shipper.

Very likely the boomer was not interested in history but the fact remains that Grays Harbor had been going strong for ten years and before that sawmills and shipyards were getting a foothold. George Stevens started it all by converting the little grist mill on the Chehalis

ORIGINAL EMERSON MILL — 1881 First plant of Northwestern Lumber Co., Hoquiam. George H. Emerson came from California to scout timber and sawmill locations for Capt. A. M. Simpson. He remained to build a mill and found a city. Alex Polson was sawyer here in 1883. (Photo Frank Eno Collection)

CITY OF HOQUIAM ABOUT 1905 Planked street ran from 8th Street bridge at right to big Hoquiam Hotel. F. G. Foster Mercantile Co. is shown in same location as present. Cattle from Montesano were unloaded at r a m p in foreground. (Photo Frank Eno Collection)

11 DAY WONDER Hoquiam's Steamer Bus was built in 1902 for passenger service to Aberdeen. On the eleventh day of operation, it fell off the road into a creek and was never salvaged. (Photo University of Washington)

GRAYS HARBOR WAS GREAT FIR PRODUCER

From the turn of the century to 1940 mills of Grays Harbor sent billions of feet of lumber to California and world ports. Top left—launching the 3-masted schooner **J. M. Weatherwax** at Aberdeen, 1890. Ship was named after sea captain who built sawmill and shipyard here in 1884. Center left, 4-masted schooner **Resolute**, built at Hitchings and Joyce shipyard at Hoquiam in 1902. Bottom left, sternwheeler **T. C. Reed**, 4-masted schooner **W. J. Patterson** and barkentine **Gleaner** at dock of Northwestern Lumber Co. Top center, S.S. **Margaret Schafer**, one of Schafer Brothers' fleet, which once carried probably record cargo of shingles—12,000 squares. At left in photo is mill of E. C. Miller Lumber Co. Bottom center, schooner at West-Slade mill No. 2. Above, S.S. **Del Norte** leaving Hoquiam. Below, barkentine **Arago** at Northwestern dock. (Photos Frank Eno Collection)

River into a sawmill. In 1881, George Emerson came from California scouting timber and sawmill locations for Capt. Asa M. Simpson, who had mills at Coos Bay and in Northern California. Emerson left but next year came back with sawmill machinery on the barkentine *Orient* and started the Northwestern Lumber Co. The next one was the Hoquiam Manufacturing Co.

In 1900 the Hoquiam Hotel reared its great bulk over the town which took another giant step in the plan and promotion of Grays Harbor City. A deepwater ship moorage was needed and the planners thought by running out a dike and building sawmills on the filled in tidelands, they would have definite advantage over the ones in the rivers. But the hotel burned to the ground and Grays Harbor City went up in another kind of smoke.

Meanwhile Aberdeen had its J. M. Weatherwax shipyard and sawmill, just west of the Wishkah River mouth. Across the river was A. J. West's plant, built in 1884. Also on the Wishkah was Emery and Mack's mill. Up in Montesano the Montesano Lumber Co. and George H. Vail were getting started.

MANSION FOR TRANSIENTS Many a visiting railroad mogul and timber baron stayed in the rambling Hoquiam Hotel. Completed in 1898, it burned to the ground in 1910. In lobby and parlor electric lights were not to be trusted and kerosene lamps were still kept in readiness. (Photo University of Washington)

CAULKS ALLOWED AT ALL TIMES Guy French's saloon in Hoquiam protected its linoleum with a steel mat but they didn't mind holes in the floor at The Lone Jack, (opposite). Just bring money. (Photo Frank Eno Collection)

In another fifteen years the sign of the "Think Of Me" cigar looked down on a changed Aberdeen and Hoquiam. They had come of age and created a lumber empire second to none anywhere. The two towns worked hard and played hard. They had a lot of good citizens but more saloons per capita than Seattle and a gang of crimps and murderers San Francisco could not touch.

In and out of Grays Harbor moved over 500 ships a year, deck-loaded with cargoes. Tugs and gulls hooted and squawked in the fog rolling up the Chehalis, Wishkah and Hoquiam Rivers. Shrieking mill whistles reminded everybody of million dollar payrolls and prosperity had come to roost. Seamen, loggers and sawmill hands swaggered across the planked sidewalks and streets, kicked their caulks in the sawdust of honky tonks, their ears ringing with the love songs of bespangled gals in knee-length skirts.

A big, new element had entered the scene — the Schafer Brothers interests. The other mills were still going strong — Anderson and Middleton, Aberdeen Lumber and Shingle, Donovan, West, Wilson Brothers, American, Federal, Western and Bay City.

In Hoquiam things were just as spectacular. Northwestern now owned a second mill in South Bend. George Kellogg was manager of E. K. Wood. When the Eureka Lumber and Shingle mill burned, Alex Polson had taken it over and put George Pauze in to run it. Other mills like Blagen's and National were whooping it up at top speed.

GALLUSES, GRITS AND GAS MANTLES as well as hardware and soft drinks could be had in Vey-sey's General Store, Hoquiam, at the turn of the century. (Photo University of Washington)

But Schafer's was something special. The three Schafer brothers, — Peter, Albert and Hubert — sons of Grays Harbor pioneers, had started logging on the Satsop River in a small way in 1893 and got a foothold. Forest fires almost wiped them out. With all their logs in a Chehalis River boom, the flood waters of 1909 would have ruined them if Pete and Albert had not stepped in as emergency crew of the tug *Edgar* (Capt. Tom Soule) and snaked the Schafer logs to safety. They recovered three-quarters of their stock while many million feet of logs belonging to others were lost over the Grays Harbor bar.

The brothers began buying up small mills in 1919 — a small one in Montesano and a bankrupt plant in Aberdeen — incorporating as Schaefer Brothers Lumber and Door Co. In 1922 the firm purchased timber, logging equipment and railroad from Grays Harbor Commercial Co. for over half a million dollars, 1928 timber of the Doty Lumber and Shingle Co. for another half million and in 1929 the timber and sawmill of Leudinghouse Brothers in Dryad for still another half million. It purchased three vessels and rechristened them *Hubert Schafer*, *Anna Schafer* and *Margaret Schafer*. At its height, Schafer Brothers were one of the largest lumbering operations in the Pacific Northwest — five mills, served by six camps, railroads, ships, tugs and three thousand employees.

GATE TO "OLD FOLKS HOME" Packing $2 suit-cases full of old newspapers, boomers and short stakers from as far east as Chicago, worked out their railroad fare at Grays Harbor Commercial Co., fabulous institution of Pope and Talbot at Cosmopolis. (Photo courtesy Stewart H. Holbrook)

HOME OF THE BRAVE AND THE FREE

It had a Greek name and the business philosophy of a rug maker. It was endowed by a king's ransom and the determination to hew to the line, letting the chips and sawdust fall on whatever heads were willing to get under it. And there were always plenty. It had more nicknames than Dutch Schultz, was ridiculed in high and low places, and not only remained impregnable but came up grinning. This was the fabulous Grays Harbor Commercial Company — Old Folks Home on the South Bank.

The name "Cosmopolis" never seemed to apply to a community or town but to a condition. It was, in effect, a sort of feudal estate where a man could wrestle lumber as long or as little as he liked at the lowest possible wage. There was no pressure attached to it and no real bitterness against the company. A man entered the gates at his own peril and could leave anytime he wished. The company had the avowed purpose of making money by cutting logs as cheaply as possible and nobody could deny that it succeeded in a monumental way. A man serving his time in this institution might find the accommodations buggy but never the management.

The Grays Harbor Commercial Company, across the Chehalis River from Aberdeen, was a Pope and Talbot property, acquired in 1888. It was a complete lumbering operation from timber to tidewater. It owned the timber, the Chehalis County Logging and Timber Railroad. It cut as much — or more — as any company in the Harbor with its sawmill, box factory, tank plant and planing mill. The stacker sheds were half a mile long. The hog farm and slaughter house were always active. The barn housed fifty horses and as many two-wheeled lumber wagons. The bakery was spacious and the cavernous mess hall seated five hundred men whose boots nestled comfortably in an inch of sawdust. There were

a dozen Chinese cooks and cookees who kept cages of ferrets for the Sunday pastime of rat hunts.

All this manorial activity was presided over for years on end by a personality who fitted the scheme of things like an oak wedge. This was Neil Cooney, bachelor extraordinary, trapshooter, duck hunter and all around show-enough satrap. The converted clubhouse overlooking the plant, was his home and showplace of the Harbor. It was filled with Japanese servants and the parties there were as gay and garish as those of another Pope and Talbot nabob — one Cyrus Walker, Lord of Ludlow, from whom Neil might have taken a cue. The difference was only in a generation or two. Where Walker has his big, brass cannon, Neil Cooney had his big, brassy Marmon.

George W. Stetson, first boss man at Cosmopolis, lured Cooney from his native heath of Port Madison to the job of mill foreman. When C. F. White became manager Neil Cooney was made superintendent, became assistant manager and finally general manager. At his right hand, which always knew what his left was doing, was office manager E. C. Stone and master mechanic was I. W. Johnson who in subsequent years founded the Grays Harbor Iron Works, which firm later became Lamb Grays Harbor Company. At one time Oscar Braunstedt was general foreman, Emil Gustafson ran the planing mill and L. B. Hogan the company store which sold everything from needles to hay.

The saying went: "If you ever go to hell, you'll find somebody who worked at Cosmopolis." If this were true, it was because the Grays Harbor Commercial Company had a "foster mother" attitude toward anybody and everybody who looked hungry. It spread its far-reaching wings over every likely job prospect in Seattle, Portland, San Francisco, Butte and Minneapolis where employment offices had standing orders to send so many "head" a week. This come-to-mama policy was not a warm-hearted

BY 1911 — STREETCARS!
8th Street Hoquiam still had planks and bicycle racks in street but trolley took you to Aberdeen on Sundays. (Photo Frank Eno Collection)

love of unfortunate humanity but simply because wages were the lowest in the business, a big labor turnover expected and planned on.

This was the Western Penitentiary into which poured a steady stream of men from the skidroads and uptown casual labor sources. Many of the recruits hired out without knowing of higher-paid jobs available but most of them were not particular or in no position to be particular. This was a "free fare" deal where drifters, boomers, derelicts, down-and-outers could eat and sleep, working temporarily without being caught at it. School-teachers, lawyers, farmers, clerks and salesmen in some kind of a bind could tide themselves over at Mr. Cooney's castle until time healed the wound. Philippinos, Japanese, Hindus — the hungry and disillusioned — come one, come all and eat table board with the moving population of Washington. They had to have baggage but they all had a home. They just had to stay long enough to work out their railroad fare and feed. Maybe a week, maybe

three days — they served their time and walked out, leaving their passports behind them — the pitiful bed rolls and pulp paper suitcases filled with old newspapers and bricks, the mountain of which overflowed the storehouse.

There never seemed to be a shortage of help at Cosmopolis. The management never seemed to care how many men left as there was a new supply swinging off every train and ship. Nor did it ever feel called upon to apologize for paying the lowest going wages. That was the way the plan operated. You took it or left for greener pastures. And there were just enough good men who stayed, got fat and warm under the protecting wing who in genuine loyalty kept the mill from panics and labor troubles. Strikes were attempted but the edges went blunt. Like Old Man River, the Old Folks Home rolled on and on making money, progress and a considerable amount of lumber.

ALOHA LUMBER CO. near Pacific Beach in Washington's Grays Harbor, organized by George Emerison, generally considered the founder of Hoquiam. (Photo University of Washington)

Burner.
Puget Mill Co. Port Ludlow, Wash.
December 1918.

FIRST WHISTLE SHRIEKED AT 5:20, second at 5:40 and you put away boiled beef, potatoes, baked beans, hash, griddle cakes, coffee and in the mill by 6. For its first 37 years the Port Gamble mill was the largest producer of Douglas fir in the world. The two schooners tied up here in 1906 were part of a vast fleet which had regular runs to California and Hawaii. (Darius Kinsey photo from Jesse E. Ebert)

FABULOUS AND FAMOUS

A Bellingham logger once lost a thousand dollar bet by refusing to believe the first lumber Pope and Talbot sold was pine. It was — from Maine, shipped out by the steamer *L. P. Foster* which also brought Andrew J. Pope, Frederic Talbot, Capt. William C. Talbot and a sawmill prefabricated in Boston. The 60 thousand feet of transported pine brought over $100 a thousand.

When the Pope and Talbot interests, which became Puget Mill Company, began sawing at Port Gamble in 1853, they were on their way to fabulous heights, to the greatest fir production of any sawmill in the world for 37 years. Sixty years later the combined companies began to lose money and so Puget Mill lost its identity to Charles R. McCormick Lumber Co. Still later this was regained — the substance if not the power and the glory.

Puget Mill did not start Washington sawmilling but did start its first lumber empire. When the *L. P. Foster* from East Machias, Maine, nosed into Puget Sound the fir was already being logged and sawed in small ways.

Hudson's Bay Co. at Fort Vancouver, Michael Simmons at Tumwater, Henry Yesler at Seattle, W. P. Sayward at Port Ludlow, J. J. Felt at Apple Tree Cove (Port

(opposite and two following pages) **SEAT OF POPE AND TALBOT EMPIRE—1918** version of Port Gamble, Wash., mill which first started sawing in 1853. Puget Mill Co. had its roots in Maine, owned by pioneers A. J. Pope, W. C. Talbot, J. P. Keller and Charles Foster. Famous, longtime general manager was Cyrus Yalker and Seattle's Dexter Horton and George Stetson worked in this mill. (Webster and Stevens photos from University of Washington)

Madison) all had little mills of uncertain finance and future. After Pope and Talbot, aided by J. P. Keller and Charles Foster with more Maine money, had started sawing, other mills took heart. One started at Seabeck, G. A. Meigs rebuilt the burned Port Madison mill to 80 thousand capacity, Amos Phinney was running the Port Ludlow mill and Capt. William Renton built his $80,000 mill at Port Blakely.

Puget Mill started at Port Gamble with a muley saw in a rough board building. Logs were hauled into the mill by cable and drum, hand spiked on the carriage. The following year production was increased six times by installing a sash saw and "live gang." The whole log passed through the saws, a chain looped around the forward end to prevent boards from slithering out over the floor. Four years later, in 1858, there was a new mill with twin circular rig, 56-inch saws cutting logs up to 9 feet in diameter. The carriage was 125 feet long and from it were coming ship spars and timbers 60 feet long.

"Little Boston" they called the village New Englanders Pope and Talbot had built. The first common labor was from the Clallam Indian tribe but there were better jobs for the few white men like George Stetson and Dexter Horton. The mill whistle woke everybody at 5:20, a second one at 5:40 was the call to boiled corned beef, potatoes, baked beans, hash, griddle cakes, biscuits, butter and coffee. At 6 work started, 11½ hours of it for $30 a month.

It was dark inside the mill at almost any hour so the owners bought dogfish oil from the Indians and burned

WHERE LUMINARIES PAID THEIR RESPECTS Admiralty Hall, mansion of Cyrus Walker. Early manager of Pope and Talbot interests at Port Ludlow had mammoth house built, as became his impressive station in life, on commanding position overlooking mill and harbor. Cannon fired salute to P&T ships. (Photo Stewart H. Holbrook Collection)

it in "tea kettle" lamps with wick in the spout on each side. The smoky flames were faint and flickering and the fishy odor took over the air of store and cookhouse as well as the mill.

The lumber went out by schooner as "venture cargoes." The super-cargo or skipper had to dispose of the boards at destination as quickly and profitably as possible. Sometimes they were sold to an agent or dealer or a plot of ground was rented and the lumber auctioned. Then a pay load of coal, sugar or passengers had to be signed up for the return voyage.

The first cargo went to Australia on the *Ella Francis* which like most of the early ships to Port Gamble was from Maine, all eventually wholly or partly owned by Puget Mill Co. — *Kaluna, Jenny Ford, Hyack, Hidalgo, Francisco, Constitution, Kutusoff, Lenore, Oak Hill, Torrent, Vernon* and *Victor*.

These were some of the vessels which got a salute from the cannon on the spacious lawn on the bluff above Port Ludlow. A second Pope and Talbot mill had been built here and a veritable potentate came as its manager in the person of Cyrus Walker and remained to rule 54 years. A mansion, Admiralty Hall, was built for him and here were entertained the great, near great and common customers if they had money or political prestige. Walker was proud of the mill and schooner fleet and when sails moved in and out of the bay, his gunner yanked the firing pin as the Stars and Stripes ran up the staff. By 1900 he was saluting the *Palmyra, Fresno, Bonanza, Carondelet, Gamble, Okanogan, Camam* and *Spokane* which had regular runs to the Philippines, Hawaii, China and Africa.

WHERE WALKER ENTERTAINED the great and near-great of "sawdust aristocracy." Pope and Talbot manager at Port Ludlow wined and dined business and political figures with pomp and ceremony. (Photo Stewart H. Holbrook Collection)

PORT LUDLOW SAWING FLOOR—1918 When the Machias, Maine, men brought their prefabricated sawmill to Port Gamble in 1853, W. P. Sayward was building a steam mill at Port Ludlow. In 1860, also on Hood Canal, Amos Phinney was cutting 60,000 feet of lumber a day. Both mills were consolidated in Puget Mill's big plant, second largest of the Pope and Talbot Empire. (Webster and Stevens photo from University of Washington)

PUGET MILL'S SECOND PLANT was at Port Ludlow, a crude beginning for this 1920 mill. By this time the company was operating at a loss and all interests had been taken over by the Charles R. McCormick Lumber Co. of Delaware, but Puget Mill regained control in 1938. (Photo from Jesse E. Ebert Collection)

BACON AND BISCUITS GOING TO CAMP from Puget Mill warehouse at Port Gamble. E. G. Ames was general manager after Cyrus Walker and company had mills at Port Ludlow, Utsalady, Port Townsend in Washington and St. Helens and Oakridge, Oregon. (Webster and Stevens photo from University of Washington)

And there were the early tugs *Resolute,* which exploded near Olympia, *Cyrus Walker, Goliah, Tyee, Yakima, Favorite* and *Wanderer* — "wood-eating, smoke-spitting aquatic threshing machines," as condemned by such sailing masters as Capt. William Gove and Capt. S. D. Libby.

But the Puget Mill prestige was to fade. During the presidency of E. G. Ames, in 1914, a contingent sale or merger was effected with Charles R. McCormick Lumber Company of Delaware which had extensive operations in Oregon and California. Puget Mill companies at the time included — Puget Sound Commercial Company, Puget Sound Tugboat Company, Puget Sound Towing Company, Rainier Investment Company, Puget Sound Cedar and Lumber Company, Grays Harbor Commercial Company, Pope and Talbot Land Company, Union River Logging Railroad Company, Admiralty Logging Company and Pacific Pine Lumber Company.

In 1938, upon failure of the McCormick interests to meet financial obligations, Puget Mill Company took over the existing interests, operating them in tune with the new era of Pacific Coast lumbering.

THEY COULD FORGE ANYTHING BUT CHECKS at this big blacksmith shop at Port Gamble. This picture was taken 50 years after the first days of muley saws and entire logs passing through gang saws with chains looped around the sawed ends to keep the boards from spilling over the floor. (Webster and Stevens photo from University of Washington)

PRAYER IN THE PLANING MILL

Maybe an early morning plant visitor would have thought there was trouble brewing. That sober-faced group of men in the office. Union stewards discussing a rule violation? Some wage demand of the boss? A protest against work conditions? None of these. T. A. Peterson was opening the plant with prayer.

The place was Onalaska, Wash., and the plant, the big Carlisle Lumber Company turning out 300 thousand feet a day. The time was any morning in the galloping '20s — any morning in any of the six days of the week.

W. A. Carlisle had hired T. A. Peterson in 1918 when he was superintendent of the Columbia River Sash and Door Co. in Rainier, Oregon. "Come on up here," Carlisle had said, this man from the South noted for its sense of hospitality. "We're big and prosperous and will pay you well and you'll have a fine, clean company town to live in. Bring your family. You'll like it."

When he got to Onalaska, between Chehalis and Morton, Peterson wasn't so sure. It was a big, booming mill all right and that was about all except the company houses and store. Nothing very inspiring about it. Well, there was a church which W. A. Carlisle had built, called the Christian Church. And T. A. Peterson, being a strongly religious man, thought that was where he belonged first of all. First things first. He was a stranger in a strange place and he wondered just why he was here. There were some odd points about his leaving that good Rainier job and coming up here where he knew no one. Could it be the hand of the Lord had reached out and put him here to help the people who needed guidance and inspiration, something to tie to? With all his modesty and self-effacing nature, Peterson thought it could be.

He took over the planing mill and found himself carrying a religious force right into the plant. During the first week he quietly asked one man here and another there if he would like to meet with others every morning before work and meditate over some chosen passage and thoughts from the Bible. It would tend to clear the way for better work and better relations with other men, sort of set the pace of goodwill for the day.

A dozen men eagerly agreed. Others thought they'd see. And most were mutely disinterested or openly scornful. But the meetings went successfully and while a few dropped out others took their place at the 7 o'clock prayers. One of these came out of curiosity but stayed to take part and returned many times. He was Kenneth C., son of the big boss. "My father thinks this is a fine idea. He's a good Presbyterian." And W. C. Carlisle expressed his own cooperation with the planing mill superintendent as an instrument of good by sending him to Tulsa, Oklahoma, to attend the national Presbyterian conference that year.

"Mr. Carlisle was an honest, forthright man," is

BURNER COMES DOWN at Pugt Mill Company's Port Ludlow, Washington, operation in 1925. Original sawmill here was built by W. P. Sayward in 1865. (Photo Ames Collection, University of Washington)

T. A. Peterson's opinion. "In most cases he did what he thought was right — not because it pleased people. And so he had trouble with the unions. Rather than accept practices he thought were detrimental, he closed the mill long before any economic factors forced him to."

So, T. A. went to Weyerhaeuser as Longview planing mill superintendent and subsequently set up his own wood specialty firm, the T. A. Peterson Manufacturing Co. "I always felt those years in Onalaska were an enriching experience for everybody who went along with us. It couldn't help but do good and we saw many evidences of it."

SCHOONERS AT MILL OF "WHITE CITY BY THE SEA." Schooners **Alvina** and **Irene** at Gardiner Mill in 1898, made famous by W. F. Jewett whose character and principles of cleanliness gave the town its color — white. (Photo courtesy Louis Seymour)

"SPOTLESS TOWN" GONE BUT NOT FORGOTTEN

White City By The Sea — Spotless Town — Jewett's Dream. In this latter day take your pick of the names they used to call it, remembering it was just another port on the broad Pacific — Gardiner, Oregon.

W. F. Jewett was the man who made the place different. His character even today pervades the creeks and valleys of the Umpqua and his spirit still presides over the faded white of the buildings on the hillside overlooking the old site of the Gardiner Mill Company.

This port three miles north of today's Reedsport had more than twenty years of history before Jewett came on the scene. In 1856 four men — Gardiner Chism, David Morey, John Kruse and George Bauer — built a mill at Barrett's Landing using timbers from the old blockhouse at Umpqua City. Then Capt. A. M. Simpson, who had been active in California, moved a redwood mill to Gardiner.

In this early day there was a mining boom up the Umpqua and Sylvester Hinsdale, of a seafaring family, came here with three Swedish wrought-iron boats equipped with steam engines and twin screws to set up river transportation to Scottsburg. He logged some for the sawmills as did Capt. Simpson's two brothers. A second mill was built by Simpson a few years later.

Then another era started in 1877 with George S. Hinsdale, Ed Breen and J. B. Leeds purchasing both mills. Two years later, Maine man W. F. Jewett appeared. Then when the Joseph Knowland interests of California bought in, Jewett became superintendent and manager, with Oscar Hinsdale second in command, and at once

instituted policies and principles that were to remain long after his death 40 years later.

The man who knows the Jewett story best is Louis Seymour who, at a hale 85, still rides the tides from his ranch into Reedsport. Louis Seymour was storekeeper at the Gardiner Mill for 43 years and was as close to

AND TRIMMERMAN PLAYED THE DRUM Everybody in the Gardiner Mill band of 1906 worked in and out of the mill. Standing, left to right— Dee Alexander, Roy Roland, Frank Spencer, Cecil Spaugh (pony sawyer), Pat Fitzgibbons, Geo. P. Stewart, Albert Janella, Louis Seymour (store manager), T. W. Angus (head sawyer), James E. Smith, Henry Bell (filer), William Lest (planerman); kneeling, left to right—Frank Seymour (teamster), J. R. Rush (trimmerman), William Bernhardt (engineer), Hopel, Sid Gilham. (Photo courtesy Louis Seymour)

SHE NAVIGATED THE UMPQUA and Winchester Bay in 1877 when George S. Hinsdale and others purchased original Gardiner Chism mill and that of Capt. A. M. Simpson, organizing Gardiner Mill Co. Louis Seymour fired Restless' wood-burning boilers. (Photo courtesy Louis Seymour)

GARDINER MILL SHIPS were an integral part of the Hinsdale-Jewett enterprise at White City By The Sea. Above, schooner Lily with 350 thousand feet of spruce for San Francisco. She usually returned with general freight and mill supplies, was sold to moving picture company for property use. Center, schooner Lucy leaving Gardiner with half a million feet of fir in 1895. Below, another Gardiner ship, Beulah, with full deck load. (Photos courtesy Louis Seymour)

W. F. Jewett as any man ever was. The mill was a lively operation when Seymour joined it after driving team in the woods at 15 and becoming chief engineer of the river steamer Restless at 22.

"People who didn't know Mr. Jewett very well," says Louis Seymour, "thought he was a ruthless driver. I guess he was — inside — with his New England conscience. But he liked everything clean and white — and he hated idleness. People around him must be busy. He probably thought I wasn't busy enough trying to keep steam up in those wood-burning boilers of the Restless and put me to work in the store. That was a long time ago and I never regretted my association with W. F. Jewett.

"The store was open from 6 in the morning until 9 at night with people in it all the time, either buying groceries or clothes or loafing and yarning around the stove. It would accommodate a lot of people — built of boiler plates and burned 4 foot slabs. Men would sit around it with their feet on the 2x4 rail and spit in the sawdust. Plug cut Star and Climax was a pretty staple item.

"Jewett's work day was as long as he was on his feet. He'd be out in the log camps as early as anybody circulating in among the Norwegians and Swedes and if a man wasn't working, he wasn't working period — not for Jewett. I remember John T. Henderson was his forester and cruiser for many years and another man who was dedicated to his work. He'd rove in a 40-mile circle buying timber, checking this tract and that, sleeping on the trail most of the time. Sam Wilson was a superintendent in the bull team days.

"And Jewett wanted everything clean around the mill, the store, houses — everywhere. Sure, this was White City — Spotless Town. I can see him now, going around without a coat picking up bits of trash that had blown in. He'd take a driver and wood wagon and comb the property. He'd even pay boys four bits a head to take a skiff and round up stray logs in the bay and river. He tried to institute this idea of cleanliness in everybody, from his daughter Narcissa Washburn Jewett and son William on down to the lowest man on the green chain. And he was always doing things to improve everybody's living like importing those three barrels of clams from his home State of Maine and planting them in the tidelands.

"He brought a love of ships with him from Maine. too. He had an interest in all the river boats around here, with Capt. Neil J. Cornwall of the steamers Eva and O. B. Hinsdale. Gardiner Mill operated several schooners and both the Lily and the Lucy were favorites of his. The company's Pasadena was the first oil-burning steam schooner on the Pacific and the San Gabriel another."

Louis Seymour likes to remember the time he first became a land owner. One summer day the schooner

STEAMER EVA WAS JEWETT'S JOY A Gardiner Mill Co. boat, the **Eva** was skippered by Capt. Neil J. Cornwall. W. F. Jewett and O. B. Hinsdale had interests in all river boats here at the turn of the century. (Photo courtesy Louis Seymour)

Lily was in and he was walking to the dock when manager Jewett hailed him, joshing about gallivanting around on the company's time. The storekeeper reminded his boss that one of his jobs was to tally ship cargo.

"All right, all right," agreed Jewett, "but I've got something more important. It's nice day. Come on up river with John and me." He referred to John Sherman Gray, head planer man and Jewett's brother-in-law. Seymour stowed the tally board and the three moved down to where Jewett had a launch tied up. "Now Louis — you be captain and I'll be the engineer. John — you do the piloting."

They went up Dean Creek, tied the boat and hiked in a mile and a quarter. A Finnish farmer, Jewett explained, wanted to sell his 160-acre ranch and he proposed the three of them buy it. Louis Seymour would manage it. "I couldn't buy a setting hen, Mr. Jewett," Louis protested, "and anyhow you've got me doing two jobs now." But they looked at the place, decided it was worth the money and that Louis Seymour's share would be $1300. "You manage the ranch," Jewett told him, "and we'll hire a man to do the actual work and pay the taxes."

"That's the way it went for about three years," says

WORKERS OF SPOTLESS TOWN TRADED HERE in Gardiner Mill Co.'s general store managed by Louis Seymour for 43 years who was a close associate of W. F. Jewett. Gardiner Mill operated from 1877 to 1918 when d e s t r o y e d by fire. (Photo courtesy Louis Seymour)

NORTH PACIFIC LUMBER MILL—PORTLAND. (Photo Oregon Collection, University of Oregon)

PORTLAND HARBOR SAWMILLS

Louis Seymour. "The ranch did all right and everybody was satisfied. Then W. F. Jewett got sick and became a sort of semi-invalid. One day Charley Douglas, a Coos Bay attorney, came up to get the Jewett accounts in shape and I signed a note for my share of the ranch. A day or so later Willy Jewett pushed his father out in the store in his wheel chair. Mr. Jewett held out his hand and gave me what was in it — the torn pieces of that note."

The Gardiner Mill burned in 1918. W. F. Jewett's son William H. built a small mill on the site, operating it for about five years. In 1938 Howard Hinsdale, son of the original Sylvester, organized the Gardiner Lumber Co. H. W. Kissling, formerly manager of Winchester Bay Lumber Co. was president, Hinsdale vice-president and J. V. Baldridge secretary. The White City of W. F. Jewett's day had lost character but the old timers could still see the man in shirt sleeves signalling the wood wagon along the hillside streets on his eternal quest for wind drift that spoiled the bayside scene.

The city boasted four bridges over the Willamette. Cows chewed their cuds on the finest lawns. Timber came down to the banks of the rivers. The Rose City was on its way to fame as a deepwater port for lumber shipping.

This was in 1895. Sawmills of one kind and another had already been active here for over forty-five years and a labor supply as well as a lumber buyers' market was well established. The whip saw plant on the river bank near Washington Street had first turned out a few boards in 1847 but two years later Col. William King built a water power mill and when it burned in 1850, W. P. Abrams and Cyrus A. Reed, a New Hampshire schoolmaster, put up a steam sawmill at Second and Stark. This was built of logs, hewn square, and men had to be brought in from neighboring areas to put them in place using a handmade derrick.

During the next ten years, two great developments took place. John West arrived from Quebec to cruise the timber on the lower Columbia and manufacture it, and the first cargo went to Sydney, Australia. After that the town of Westport never ceased making lumber. Also young John Halsey Jones left his job as a Clatskanie logger, walked to Portland, invested his savings in a sawmill site on Cedar Creek and with his father, Justus Jones, built a dam and erected a crude sawmill. The single sash,

STEAM SCHOONER "MONTAGUE" LOADS at Portland. (Photo Oregon Collection, University of Oregon)

up-and-down saw as well as the carriage was run by water power, the rough lumber, mostly cedar, hauled to Portland by ox team and wagon.

In a short while the Jones were able to buy acreage in the old Terwilliger claim and build a steam sawmill, the machinery for which came from New York, partly around the Horn and partly trucked across the Isthmus of Panama. Word got around from house to trading post that "people these days are gettin' pretty high and mighty. Some new-fangled kind of explosive machinery is goin' in that new mill. They better watch what they're a-doin'." But the boilers didn't blow up and the mill cut 15 thousand feet a day which meant in twelve or fourteen hours.

The elder Jones was a thrifty man. John Halsey started to buy oil for the machinery. "Oil?" roared Justus, "We got along with bacon rinds on the muley saw at Cedar Creek. Oil!" But oil they used — on steel gears, not fir plugs. The logs came from Sellwood, across the Willamette, this part of Portland then covered with dense stands of fir and hemlock. The sawmill men were all-purpose crews, stopping the machinery to cross the river by boat, fell and buck trees into logs which they made up into rafts, towed to the mill by their rowboat.

In 1864 the sawmill burned to the ground. It was rebuilt at once. In 1879 fire razed it again. Once more it was reconstructed, bigger and better. Dry kilns were installed in 1899 — the first in the district. In 1905 the

FRONT STREET MILL—PORTLAND about 1905. (Photo Tillamook Pioneer Museum)

YARD AND MILL—PORTLAND LUMBER COMPANY. (Photo Oregon Collection, University of Oregon)

mill had Portland's first band saw and in 1911 its first gasoline truck although lumber was hauled for many years following by the Jones Lumber Company's thirty head of draught horses.

Several small mills sprang up from Portland to the sea in the early '70s. Then George W. Weidler built a mill at the foot of Savier Street and cut 50 thousand feet a day. This "wonder of the ages" brought the curious from near and far. The district became known as Slabtown and the operation eventually became the Willamette Steam Sawmills and Manufacturing Co.

The Knapp steam mill at Knappton, which was later to emerge as the Peninsula Lumber Company, was bought by Capt. A. M. Simpson and shipped to Empire on Coos Bay. Pennoyer's plant later became Portland Lumber Co. In 1879 Simon Benson arrived to start logging around St. Helens.

In 1895 M. F. Henderson and Lucky Jack Peterson leased a tract of land near Portland, built a sawmill and launched the Western Lumber Company, the name changed as developments occurred to Eastern and Western Lumber Company. Winslow B. Ayer had been operating the Portland Cordage Company, became partner as Peterson left to go logging.

In 1903 F. H. Ransom came from Sierra Lumber Company in California to become manager and the company bought timber west of Kelso and on Westport Slough and when it took over the small circular mill of Albina Lumber Company, its owner W. A. Dempsey became secretary of Eastern and Western. Phillip Buehner was assistant manager.

One May night of this year, just after the six p.m. whistle, while workers were lined up for their pay envelopes, two men moved out of the black fog with their faces masked and held up the office, escaping with the $5000 payroll. A few days later fire destroyed the old Western mill.

Eastern and Western Lumber Company used a sawmill without a green chain. A "camelback" conveyor pulled all lumber out into the yard where it slithered to either side and formed a mountainous heap. The plan seemed to be to get it out of the mill as quickly as possible so more could be cut. Many times an order could not be filled because it was impossible to sort out the sizes and grades from the big pile and it was necessary to cut it again, perhaps a third time. In this haphazard system, or lack of it, sawmill hands often left the job to catch trout in the creek which ran through a gulch nearby.

Labor unrest centered on Eastern and Western. In March, 1906, J. W. Fowler became the new superintendent. The sawmill workers demanded a raise and Fowler told them to wait. No decision forthcoming, the men walked off the job. Other mills went on strike with Big Bill Haywood heading the organizing. There was a constant parade of strikers at the Eastern and Western plant, fighting, stone throwing. Fifteen police officers were assigned duty here while I.W.W. members made off with the strike fund.

Close by the Eastern and Western mill one night, moving along in the dark waters of the Willamette River, a beautiful maiden was dimly seen clinging to the bark of a big log while a terror stricken man clawed his way to the top of a giant sawdust pile and leaped to his death. Thus was justice and retribution depicted in filming the climax of James Oliver Curwood's "The Flaming Forest."

HAMMOND LUMBER MILL—GARIBALDI on Tillamook Bay, Ore., in 1929. (Photo Tillamook County Pioneer Museum)

THREE WHISTLES SAVED THE MILL

The skipper of the *Santa Maria* was afraid of the Tillamook Bar. He said so. He accepted the lumber cargo and the farewell honors tendered him but doubted if he'd ever be back to this sawmill. He'd see. When he got to deep water, he'd sound the ship's whistle — one long blast if he stood on his better judgment not to return, three short ones if he decided to return.

The mill was shut down while everybody in Hobsonville stood or climbed the cliffs to watch the *Santa Maria* cross out. When at long last she was safely out of the Bay and heading south, all eyes were fastened to the whistle bolted to her stack. Their jobs depended on what the steam jet said. Then a white plume shot out and rode away on the southwest wind. Nothing more. All hearts sank. The *Santa Maria* was not coming back. Then suddenly a second wisp of steam appeared. And a third. The crew threw hats in the air and danced on them. Joseph Smith bellowed above the noise: "Get up steam and saw like hell! We got to have lumber ready when she docks again!"

This was the high point in the early career of the Hobsonville, Oregon, sawmill. The 1886 incident set it on a firm business footing and for twenty years it thrived under several owners, eventually drifting into a long period of inactivity and suspense, being finally abandoned to rats and rust.

The Joseph Smith family started the famous mill operation. In 1883, Smith and his two husky sons tried to buy a sawmill site from Charles Robson, founder and principal landowner of Hobsonville. They considered the water carry from Astoria to Tillamook Bay and decided a mill here, shipping direct to San Francisco, would have a definite advantage. But Robson had no sites to sell. The Smiths then blasted one of the rock on the point, extending it on piling.

Then their troubles began. Machinery ordered from Astoria had to be rescued from flames in the great fire of July 2, 1883. Then the ship carrying it south was wrecked on the Tillamook Bar and the equipment was badly damaged when salvaged. When the mill did get started there was only the scanty local market of Lincoln (later Tillamook) and Hobsonville to supply.

The Smiths had only one element in their favor — labor. The crew was made up of homesteaders and Indians whose wages were paid with orders on the company store. There were bunkhouses for Indian bucks and single white men. The men with families built shanties on the rocky shelves above the mill. A sawmill town grew up on the terraced ground on both sides and a hotel site blasted out of the cliff. A lumber yard was built and the slab incline running from beach to cliff top was dubbed Sawdust Avenue.

With the mill sawing, Joseph Smith negotiated with San Francisco for space on boats for direct shipment.

TILLAMOOK BAY CLASSIC AT HOBSONVILLE 1899 look at Truckee Lumber Co. mill, built and first operated by Joseph Smith and sons in 1883 under severe difficulties. Hadley Lumber Co. bought mill in 1906, next year reorganizing as Miami Lumber Co. In 1909 it was sold to Ganahl and Co. of San Francisco but soon lay idle. Watchman held vigil for ten years but mill went into decay. (Photo Tillamook County Pioneer Museum)

PROSPERITY RULED OVER KRUGER SHIPS when they carried lumber to San Francisco for Truckee Lumber Co. at old Hobsonville. Left to right in photo—sea tug **Ranger**, steam schooners **W. H. Kruger** and **Truckee**, bay tug **Annarine** docked at company store. (Photo Tillamook County Pioneer Museum)

But California ship owners were afraid of the Tillamook Bar. Impatiently Smith sent his son "Buck" south with power to buy, lease or otherwise procure ships — even if he had to mortgage the sawmill to do it. It was not until 1886 that Buck Smith was able to lease a steamer, the *Santa Maria* and he returned on her as pilot. Then came the high drama recounted above and the mill went ahead, employing forty men with high hopes.

Two years later the Smiths sold out to the Truckee Lumber Company of California and with W. H. Krueger at his head and J. E. Sibley in charge of the sawmill, the enterprise went on to expansion and glory. With the company's own ships crossing the bar successfully other skippers called for cargoes. The five hundred people in

HOBSONVILLE MILL CREW—1890. Left to right: "1 — Archie Gish, 2 — Paul Thorall, 3—Frank Pierson, 4—Lester Nilson, 5—Hewey Robbins, 6—Conrad Thorall, 7—Jim Mapes, 8—Bill Gilmore, 9—Wm. Campbell, 10 —called "The Tramp," 11— John Bodle, 12—Bob Robbins, 13—Theo. Jacoby, 14— Lee Alley, 15—Al Bynum, 16—Joe Warren, 17—.......... McDonald, 18—Ben Benton, 19—Lew. Riefenberg, 20— Ben Vantress, 21 — Harold Weaver, 22 — Phineas Vantress, 23—Harry Warren, 24 — Billy Watt, 25 — Frank Warren, 26—Andy Williams, 27—Pat Doughney, 28—unidentified, 29—Jimmie Heedspeth, 30—Milo Richardson, 31 — unidentified, 32 — Geo. Allendorf, 33—Gust Nelson, 34 — J. E. Sibley." (Photo Tillamook County Pioneer Museum)

Hobsonville saw its highest prosperity during the next seventeen years. Krueger died early in this period and O. C. Haslett became president, building the steamers *W. H. Krueger* and *Redondo* for the California trade. The *Sequoia*, also operated by the Truckee Lumber Company, was wrecked on the Bar with a full cargo of lumber.

From 1906 to 1909 the mill had three owners — then obscurity. Local interests formed the Hadley Lumber Company which took over the mill, changing the firm name to Miami Lumber Company. Then a business depression closed the plant and then Ganahl and Company of San Francisco attempted to operate it with no success.

Then followed a long period of suspense and waiting. The mill crew remained for a while, hoping against hope

the operation would be resumed, but finally drifted away, one by one. A watchman was retained to look after the property and year after year, he and his wife, living over the once busy store, saw the mill deteriorate. The buildings fell into disrepair, the logs broke out of booms in the winter storms. The hotel remained furnished but no one came to stay in it.

For ten long years the watchman's lonely vigil went on. Then came complete abandonment. The mill buildings became bare bones with tree shoots growing between the slabs of the sawing floor. Rats scampered over the cookhouse range, docks and booms. Rust ate the refuse burner away. Hobsonville had a ghost.

EFFENBERGER MILL — NEHALEM about 1905. Left to right: Otto Effenberger, Oscar Effenberger, Dave Peregoy, Walter Walker, Bill Effenberger, Joe Effenberger, Oscar Kline. (Photo Tillamook County Pioneer Museum)

BROOKINGS HAD A SAWMILL

At ten o'clock in the morning of a day that held much promise, the mill whistle suddenly sounded and extended into a long, drawn-out, apprehensive howl. Perhaps half a dozen people in Brookings knew what the whistle meant. Most of the townspeople and workers in the big California and Oregon Lumber Company mill simply wondered. Within minutes they knew.

The C and O whistle on that 1925 day sounded the end of hopes, plans and operation. The mill machinery stopped with a jolt. Not another wheel or roll ever turned. A redwood log lay sprawled halfway up the slip. The carriage jerked to a standstill just before it came up to the slack band saw. Fires died under the boilers. Ships at the long dock rocked idly, short of cargo. Crane arms pointed at varying angles. Cedar, spruce and redwood in the pond remained undisturbed as green lumber warped in the yards. This was it.

The California and Oregon Lumber Company had been launched in a big way with all the backing wealth could give it, with all the confidence and cooperation of grateful citizens. But after eleven years of operation errors of judgment and management had caught up and a great enterprise was a dead thing. Within a week 1100 people moved out of Brookings, hotels and stores closed and the mill lay victim to the ravaging reach of rust and decay.

The Brookings story goes back to 1906 when William James Ward, fresh out of Cornell and the Forestry Service, cruised timber along the Pistol and Chetco

HOPES WERE HIGH IN 1914 when this picture was taken of new California and Oregon Lumber Co. mill in Brookings, Ore., but blasted when mill suddenly shut down in 1925 and never reopened. (Photo courtesy L. P. Cress)

THERE WAS BIG MONEY behind the Brookings boom that began in 1906 when the Brookings family of San Bernardino, Calif., acquired extensive timber lands in Curry County. (Photo courtesy L. P. Cress)

Rivers. He had been sent here by the Brookings family —
John E., Robert S. and W. Dubois — which operated
the successful San Bernardino Lumber and Box Company
and had endowed the Brookings Institute in Washington, D.C.

With the purchase of timber the California and Oregon enterprise began. Nothing was too good, said the
Brookings men. They brought in expert designers to
plan and place the mill properly. Hotels, stores, workers'
homes were built. A bank opened. Thirty miles of railroad tapped the redwoods and a thousand foot dock ran
out to meet the ships.

L. P. "Vern" Cross was one of the men who had come
up from "San Berdoo" to work at the new mill. He ran
an engine on the woods grade. He remembers vividly
the 1914 day when the mill opened and the future was
bright. After the blow up he was one of the few who
stayed in town.

"We had a lot of good years and never a hint that
things weren't going right with management. Henry
Nutting was woods superintendent and James H. Owen
mill manager. J. E. Brookings' son Walter was sales
manager in the San Francisco office. I brought in many
a trainload of logs and there were ships in here all the
time, company owned — the *Brookings, Quinault, South
West, Stout*. They carried rough lumber to the finishing
plant at C and O yard in Oakland. Frank Stout held the
controlling interest after 1920 and Mr. Gray was manager then.

"It was all too good to be true, I guess. Sure was a
big disappointment to all of us when the mill closed.
I was just braking down for the mill with twenty-eight
cars of logs when that mournful old whistle started.
Figured something unusual was up. Didn't take me long
to find out I had no more job.

"Then the depression really finished things here until
the town began to make a normal comeback. The Brookings Land and Timber Company began liquidating all
its interests. The bank closed. That was the last straw."

But human nature is innately hopeful. The big bulk
of the mill still stood there on the bluff and people still
looked at it and thought maybe it would start up again.
"You never know how big business figures things. Other
mills here on the Coast are doing all right."

Then they had an answer and it was not good. They
saw two men go into the mill one morning and when
they came out, smoke followed them. And then flames.
The big mill was burning up. The townspeople watched
it burn with sad eyes and the two workmen shrugged off
questions. They just had orders to burn the mill. Only
way to stop the taxes.

Brookings had a lumber industry — it says here.

1000 FOOT DOCK SERVED C&O SHIPS California and Oregon Lumber Co. owned carriers **Brookings, Quinault, South Coast, Stout** and other ships freighting lumber to remanufacturing plant in Oakland. The **Brookings** had been a Great Lakes ore boat. (Photo courtesy L. P. Cress)

30 MILES OF RAILROAD tapping timber in the Pistol and Chetco River areas was one of the high costs of California and Oregon Lumber Co. operation in Brookings. Company also owned ships and planned great future for the town. L. P. "Vern" Cross, donor of these pictures, was engineer here. (Photo courtesy L. P. Cross)

SCHOONER KLICKITAT was one of fleet on the regular run between Port Gamble, California and Hawaii. Twelve foot deck loads were customary cargo and more than often were swept overboard before ships cleared Cape Flattery. (Photo Ames Collection, University of Washington)

LUMBER ON THE HIGH SEAS

At the turn of the century tall masts and taut lines screened every harbor on the Coast between San Francisco and Vancouver. In every cove boasting a sawmill, sail-borne ships lay in wait for cargo or were loading it by hand. And wherever there were tidewater mills little shipyards were bending keels for wooden lumber carriers large and small. Gold and oil in California, rebuilding San Francisco after the fire, building the Panama Canal and the first World War gave tremendous impetus to the lumber industry. California coastal shipyards, Coos Bay, the Columbia River, Hoquiam, Aberdeen, Port Blakely, Winslow, Tacoma, Everett, Bellingham, Victoria and Vancouver contributed vessels to carry it. Ballard, just outside of Seattle, also built schooners for the trade — among them the *Wilbert L. Smith, William Nottingham, Willis A. Holden, J. W. Clise* and *Alex T. Brown.*

The three-master schooner *C. A. Thayer,* built at Fairhaven, California, in 1895, was a long-lived example of the sturdiness of Douglas fir for ships. With a capacity of 575,000 feet of lumber she was comparatively large — length, 156 feet; beam, 36 feet; depth 11.8 feet; 452 tons gross.

Until World War II the schooners *Commodore*, built in Seattle in 1919, and *Vigilant,* built in Hoquiam in 1920, were regularly engaged in the lumber carrying trade from the Pacific Northwest to the Hawaiian Islands for the firms of Lewers & Cooke and City Mill Co. The former ship carried 1,500,000 feet, the latter 1,700,000. They were the last of the big windjammers which lent great romance to the waterfront.

To Hawaii also sailed the four-masted schooner *Alice Cooke,* built at Port Blakely in 1891. She preceded the *Commodore* in plying this route carrying 900,000 feet each voyage. Other well known sailers built from 1918 to 1920 for carrying lumber included the *Betsy Ross, Ecola, K. V. Kruse, L. W. Ostrander, Malahat, Monitor, North Bend, Oregon Fir, Oregon Pine, George U. Hind, S. P. Tolmie, Fort Laramie, Ella A., Eleanor H., Forest Dream, Forest Pride, Forest Friend, Conqueror, Anne Comyn* and *Katherine McCall.* While they made profit for their owners during lumbers big heyday they fell victims to the post-war depression and the competition of steam.

Actually ships built on the West Coast constituted only a small part of the tonnage calling there for cargoes.

BUILDING DECKLOAD ON SCHOONER at Warren, Oregon. (Weister Co. photo from Oregon Collection, University of Oregon)

Most of these were British and European. One of the most unique was the seven-masted iron barkentine *E. R. Sterling*, built in Belfast in 1883 and launched as the *Columbia* for German owners. About 1907 the vessel was wrecked off the Washington coast and after being salvaged was admitted to American register and rebuilt as a seven-master with square sails on her foremast. This unusual rig attracted attention in every port and there were plenty of them from the North Pacific to Australia — 2,500,000 feet of lumber out, coal on the return voyage.

Other big sailers were those of the Dollar fleet, most of them previously German owned and war captured. The *Alexander Dollar* and some of the others carried 3,000,000 feet or more. Of the large wooden carriers the *Oregon Fir* and *Oregon Pine*, five-masters built on the Columbia in 1920, had a capacity of 2,400,000 feet.

Fifty years ago lumber was hauled to shipside by horse and hand truck, slid down a chute by gravity or lifted aboard in slingload by gear operated by a donkey. The rough lumber was piled solid and it took time and much labor to stow and unload. It also required many long days to get these windjammers over the seas. Yet many of the voyages equalled steamship time of later date. The barkentine *Irmgard* made the trip from Hono-

lulu to San Francisco in 10 days and 10 hours and the barkentine *Annie Johnson* made the reverse trip in 8 days and 18 hours, log book showing her top speed at 13 knots, none less than 9. The schooner *Spokane* once made the Honolulu to Cape Flattery run — 2,288 miles — in 8 days and 16 hours. The schooner *Solano* ran from Shanghai to Port Townsend in 24 days.

The steam schooner was a type developed on and for the North Pacific, designed for the rapid handling of lumber. Many of the early carriers were "single enders" with engines and housing aft, affording an entire sweep of the deck for long lengths and permitting speed in loading and discharging. In those days a carrier of 500,000 feet was in the large class. As capacities increased to a million and a million and a half designs were altered to fit all types of lumber cargoes.

Plans for the typical steam schooner called for ample stability with about two-fifths of the cargo in the hold. three-fifths as deck load. Consequently these handy and useful craft looked like floating lumber stacks when outward bound. One fact that promoted the single-end type was that with machinery aft, they could nose into small, shallow harbors where ships on even keel could not reach. The newer type of steam schooner carried long wooden booms, 70 to 75 feet in length, which

TWO-TON TIMBERS FOR TEUTONS Loading bridge timbers through stern ports of German schooner **Lilbek** at Port Blakely about 1910. Timbers sized 22″x22″x79′. (Asahel Curtis photo from Washington State Historical Society)

reached to the end of loading docks, eliminating labor and moving berth. Further fast handling was attained by winches with offshore and inshore falls operated by one driver. Double-enders were later equipped with fast gear fore and aft, some ships with runways through the midship house for long timbers on deck.

When chartered for lumber, many foreign-built ships with short decks and small hatches had to have their fore and aft ports cut so that long lengths of timbers and piling could be loaded. Vessels built for the trade had expanded hatches and long deck space making port unnecessary.

Some of the power vessels catering to the lumber trade were the *Brookdale, Donna Lane, Caoba, Lake Francis, La Merced, Libby Maine, Mount Baker, Nika,*

Oregon, Redwood, W. F. Barrows, H. B. Lovejoy, J. C. Kirkpatrick, Joanna Smith, Santa Flavia, Sierra, Skagway and *Frank Lynch.*

To the above memory adds the name of steamer schooners which made West Coast History: *Nehalem, Necanicum, F. S. Loop, Horace X. Baxter, Hornet, Wasp, Bee, Johan Poulsen, Santa Ana, Santa Inez, Culburra, Cethana, Boobyalla, Mukilteo,* barge *Rufus E. Wood, Wilmington, Nome City, Multnomah, Port Angeles, Lakme, Falcon, Charles Nelson, Cricket, Davenport, Norwood, Fred Baxter, Providencia, Tiverton, Hartwood, Parsis O, Svea, Willie A. Higgins, Frank D. Stout, Pasadena, Phoenix, Rosalie Mahoney, Wapama, Wahkeena, G. C. Landauer, Helen P. Drew, J. B. Stetson, Ernest H. Meyer, Elizabeth* and *San Diego.*

MADE 80 DAY WARTIME VOYAGE with 1,590,000 feet of lumber from mills of MacMillan and Bloedel, Limited. Five-masted **City Of Alberni,** built at Hoquiam, Wash., sailed from Vancouver to Sidney, Australia, encountering storms, intense heat and enemy threats, but made 9000 mile trip safely. (Photo from MacMillan and Bloedel, Limited, Collection)

SHE PADDLED LOGS AND LUMBER Working out of Everett, Washington, the sternwheeler **Swinomish** was once assigned to haul a scowload of lumber out to an English bark. The mate of the "limejuicer" saw the **Swinomish** belching smoke, her deck house almost hidden by piles of lumber. "I say, sir," he said to the captain, "this is an odd country. They bring the sawmill right out to the ship!" (Photo Joe Williamson Collection)

EMPIRE MILL RESISTED STORMS of wind, weather and commerce. Built of Port Orford cedar on heavy piling, mill at Empire City, Coos Bay, was effort of Southern Oregon Improvement Co. to carry on original business built by Henry H. Luse. Mill remained idle for 40 years while crew kept machinery oiled. (Photo Victor C. West Collection)

BAY CITY MILL HAS HAD VARIED CAREER
This Coos Bay veteran was originally operated by Labree in early '80s, then by Merchant until Dean Lumber Co. took it over. In 1907 C. A. Smith Lumber Co. ran mill, later selling to McKenna Lumber Co. Latest owner Coos Head Timber Co. (Photo Victor C. West Collection)

COOS BAY GOES SAWMILLING

They were saying around the settlement, where the Coos River formed a bay in the Pacific Ocean, there was a race on between a man named Luse and a Capt. Simpson as to which would get his sawmill finished first. Either way it looked like things were going to be good. There was lots of timber around, a good deepwater harbor inside the bar and men would have a lot of work.

Here in Coos Bay in 1856 there wasn't much to get excited about. Capt. William H. Harris, a member of the Coos Bay Company which explored the area a few years before, had decided to stay. He took up a donation land claim, made a trip to Roseburg to file it and returned to build a cabin. He laid out the town and platted eight blocks of it, called it Empire because it sounded big. A hotel was built, a store appeared and a fort was built to discourage the Indians.

Now both Henry Luse and Capt. Simpson were livening things up. Luse was an intelligent and energetic pioneer who had educated himself through study and reading. He saw all the timber and wanted to do something about it. When he heard of a sawmill for sale in Astoria, he went there and brought it back to Empire where Capt. Harris gave him land on the waterfront.

Capt. Asa M. Simpson had walked up from California, bought 160 acres of land and timber for $300 and started the framework of a sawmill. Then he went back south, bought the machinery used in gold pioneer Sutter's mill, loaded it on the coaster *Quadratus* and with his brother, Louis P. Simpson, started north.

Henry Luse's mill was almost finished when the *Quadratus* tried to cross the Coos Bay bar in a storm. She struck a reef and with seas sweeping over her decks

several men were lost including Louis Simpson. But finally the *Quadratus* was blown free and managed to limp into Empire with the machinery intact. Then Capt. Asa found to his dismay that Henry Luse's mill was already operating.

It was a steam mill cutting 8 to 10 thousand feet every twenty-four hours. Luse himself worked as long as eighteen, in the mill or salvaging logs off the beach, since he had spent all his cash on the mill.

During the 1860s both Luse and Simpson built shipyards, the latter turning out 58 ships, one of them the first full-rigged vessel built on the Pacific Coast — the *Western Shore*. Luse improved his sawmill and built wharves beyond the mud flats, linking them to the mill with a trestled approach on which ran a tram. Warehouses went up and business thrived. The Port Orford cedar brought a premium price in San Francisco to be made into lucifer matches and broom handles, lath and

STAVE MILL WAS COOS BAY OLD TIMER— built about 1900 and operated by Oakland Box and Stave Co. (Photo Victor C. West Collection)

ORIGINAL PORTER MILL PRESENT WEYERHAEUSER PLANT Built by California Lumber Co. in 1880, mill became Capt. A. M. Simpson's second Coos Bay property in 1899. Buehner Lumber Co. operated it, then Stout Lumber Co. until it burned on Feb. 25, 1926. Shipyard shown is Kruse and Banks. Mound at left held grave of Indian chief, each owner preserving it until Weyerhaeuser enlarged plant. (Photo Oregon Historical Society)

SIMPSON'S FIRST IN COOS BAY "Old Town" sawmill built in 1858 by Capt. Asa Simpson in competition with Henry Luse as to which mill would be finished first. Simpson lost when ship **Quadratus** bringing equipment of Sutter's California mill was wrecked on Coos Bay bar. Asa Simpson's brother Louis P. was lost, machinery saved. Under several owners mill had 93 years' operation. (Photo Victor C. West Collection)

staves. Empire became the Coos County seat and rated a customs house.

Both sawmills had economic trouble and were plagued by fires. After the one in 1885, Capt. Simpson bought out brother Robert, changed the firm name to Simpson Lumber Company, enlarged the mill and made son Louis J. Simpson president.

About this time Empire got a new lease on life when the Southern Oregon Improvement Company bought Henry Luse's sawmill and acquired 170 town lots. Big plans were made and included a railroad from Roseburg. Machinery for a monster mill was ordered from the East and two steamers came around the Horn to be used in trade.

Work was begun on the mill on a broad scale. Four piledrivers drove 4000 white cedar piles and for the mill building itself which was 72'x400', 364 additional piles were sunk and capped by 13"x16" timbers. Floor joists were 6"x16", uprights 16"x16" supporting stringers of the same size.

However the plans met snags. The railroad from Roseburg never materialized and Empire was not considered as good for shipping as North Bend and Marshfield. Columbia River ports had already captured most of the market. The mill closed down but the owners kept it ready to saw lumber at any moment. For forty years the maintenance crew oiled and greased the machinery. Some of them died of old age and were replaced. When

STEAM SCHOONER A. M. SIMPSON loads door stock at plant of North Bend Manufacturing Co. (Photo Oregon Historical Society)

113

the whistle finally blew the mill was ready and the saws hummed, thanks to Port Orford cedar and patience.

In the meantime Simpson's Old Town mill as they called it in Marshfield and North Bend, was taken over by other owners, in succession — Bay Park Lumber Company, McDonald-Vaughan (William Vaughan had worked as Simpson's bookkeeper) and Coos Bay Logging Company of which Vaughan was president.

In 1899 Capt. Simpson acquired the sawmill of the California Lumber Company, which was known as the Porter Mill. This also had a parade of owners over the years, among them — Buehner Lumber Company and Stout Lumber Company. It burned on Feb. 25, 1926. Each new owner rebuilt and enlarged the mill, the last one Weyerhaeuser Timber Co.

After the turn of the century another mill enterprise put Coos Bay in the big time. A Minneapolis lumberman, C. A. Smith, who had been operating in Eldorado County (Calif.) sugar pine, Humboldt County redwood (Bay Meadows) and Oregon spruce on the Alsea River, bought timber back of Coos Bay and set up the Smith-Powers Logging Co.

The next step was the purchase of a small sawmill at the head of Coos Bay — the Dean Mill — which later became known as the East Side Mill. Across the inlet Smith bought a large tract of land and built the main sawmill. Finishing plant was at Bay Point, Calif. and steam schooners *Nann Smith* and *Redondo* shuttled between, making round trips every five days. A third ship, *Adeline*, was added to the fleet in 1912.

CALLED "LARGEST SAWMILL IN WORLD" in 1912 by newspapers—C. A. Smith Lumber Co., Marshfield, Ore. Minneapolis lumberman Smith purchased Dean mill, rebuilt nearby and with steamers **Nann Smith** and **Redondo** running to finishing plant at Bay Point, Calif., had mammoth operation. (Photo Victor C. West Collection)

At this time the payroll included about 2000 names. The Portland Oregonian called the C. A. Smith Lumber Company "the largest sawmill in the world" and the American Lumberman issued a special 100 page supplement lauding the operation in all detail. Smith-Powers Logging Co. owned 220,000 acres in Coos and Douglas Counties, almost all Port Orford cedar. And C. A. Smith, always a business man, purchased a ranch, primarily for the timber, but the first year the land yielded 9000 boxes of strawberries and 600 boxes of apples.

"MILL B" WAS ANOTHER COOS BAY STALWART Plant of North Bend Manufacturing Co. was formerly Stout mill, then owned by Irwin-Lyons and Al Pierce Lumber Co. (Photo Oregon Historical Society)

20 MILLION FEET of redwood logs in this Pudding Creek winter storage. From 1906 to 1916, Union Lumber Co. removed logs by incline and railroaded them one mile to mill at Fort Bragg. (Photo Union Lumber Company Collection)

MENDOCINO COUNTY HAS COLORFUL PAST

The first attempts at lumbering along the Northern California coast were in the early '50s. Chinese had rigged up perpetually-operating muley saws powered by incoming and outgoing tides. Settlers crossing the Humboldt Bar, beached the side-wheel steamer *Santa Clara* near the future towns of Buckport and Arcata and with long belts hitched up to the ship's paddle wheels got power to four saws on shore, cutting 40,000 feet of redwood a day.

A small water power mill was built on the Albion River by Capt. William Richardson in 1851; another was a larger, steam-powered mill on Big River in 1852, with a second mill built to handle the bigger redwoods just north of the present Mendocino City. The latter enterprises were known as the California Lumber Co. and owned by Harry Meiggs, Jerome Ford and E. C. Williams.

The Big River mill burned in 1863, was rebuilt and operated until 1938. Another steam mill was built on the Albion River in 1853, owned in 1856 by A. W. MacPherson a native of Scotland, who took in a partner, Henry Wetherby, and rebuilt the mill when it burned in 1867. These two men later organized the Pacific Lumber Co. in Humboldt County. When MacPherson died in 1880, the Albion property became the Albion Lumber Co. which was sold to Miles Standish (an actual descendant of Pilgrim Capt. Miles Standish) and Henry Hickey, who after 15 years, sold the mill to the Southern Pacific Railroad, which operated it until 1929.

Another early redwood sawmill was started by George Hagenmayer on the Noyo River in 1852. The Indians interfered with its operation and high water two years later carried the buildings out to sea. Inland a water power sawmill was constructed by John Gshwond in 1856 at the west end of Anderson Valley over a fork of the Navarro River. Other mills were built on the same

115

FIRST STEEL WHEEL on band saw head rig in redwoods. In the 90's, C. R. Johnson, founder of Union Lumber Company, braved ridicule in introducing band saws which first used wooden wheels. Arm at left controlled belt to wheel, was hinged to clear big redwood logs. (Photo Union Lumber Company Collection)

INCLINE TO SCHOONER
Redwood lumber at Greenwood C r e e k was lowered down t h i s narrow gauge incline and loaded on ships by c h u t e. S c h o o n e r is **Whitesboro.** (Photo Union L u m b e r Company Collection)

(Pages 116 and 117) **GIANT S L I C E S FOR SHINGLE BOLTS** Bucking crew cutting and splitting redwood monarch. (Photo courtesy Hammond- California Redwood Company)

vicinity by the Clow brothers, Thomas Hiatt and H. O. Irish.

From 1858 onward several small mills were established in the interior portion of Mendocino county — by Thomas Elliott, in Redwood Valley, G. F. Bennett near Laytonville, E. Pryor on Ackerman Creek, Stephen Holden near Ukiah, Hiram Hatch at Sherwood Valley, Andrew Gray near Covelo, and the Blosser Bros., near Willits.

The distinction of a sawmill operating on the oldest mill site goes to the Caspar Lumber Company. About 1860, Kelley and Randall built a mill on Caspar creek. Jacob G. Jackson, a native of Vermont, bought into the firm which was operated as the Caspar River Mills.

Fire levelled the Caspar sawmill in 1889, but it was rebuilt and resumed operations in 1890. Jackson died in 1901, and was succeeded in the company management by his daughter, Mrs. Annie Krebs, and later by his grandsons, C. E. DeCamp and C. J. Wood.

The forerunner of another historic sawmill started

in 1861 when Tichenor and Hendy built a mill at the mouth of the Navarro river. In 1863 Tichenor bought out Hendy, and continued as H. B. Tichenor and Company. Later Robert Byxbee bought into the company and when Tichenor died, formed a partnership with Joseph Clark known as the Navarro Lumber Company. The sawmill burned in 1890, was rebuilt and burned again in 1902, ending a 40 year career during most of which it was one of the leading producers of Mendocino redwood.

In 1903 a new sawmill was completed at Wendling (now Navarro), about 15 miles up the Navarro river from its mouth. This mill, operated by the Wendling Milling and Lumber company, was purchased in 1905 by the Stearns Lumber company. Stearns ceased to operate in 1912, and the next year the mill and timber were purchased by the Standish and Hickey interests, after which it operated as the Navarro Lumber company. In 1920 the Albion Lumber company bought out the Navarro Lumber company, acquiring a second redwood

ROLLING REDWOOD THE HARD WAY in the old days at Fort Bragg. It was slow work and not always sure—moving logs by jackscrews in 1890. (Photo Union Lumber Company Collection)

sawmill for the Southern Pacific Land company. The Navarro mill was operated through 1927.

The year 1862 marks the beginning of another sawmill on a site in use today. John Rutherford and George Webber built a steam mill at the mouth of the Gualala river. William Heywood and S. H. Harmon purchased half interest in this mill in 1868, and by 1872 had complete control. The Gualala Mill company was formed four years later consisting of two new men, Charles Dingley and William Bihler in addition to Heywood and Harmon. In 1903 the Empire Redwood company purchased the Gualala mill. This mill was destroyed by fire in 1906.

The E. B. Salsig company, which had purchased the timber of Empire Redwood company, started construction of a new mill on the Gualala river in 1914. The following year the property was taken over by the American Redwood company, which continued construction of the mill. In 1920, the National Redwood company took over for a while. The mill was idle from 1921 through 1938 then operated from 1939 through 1942 as Gualala Lumber company, leased part of that time by the Southern Redwood company. The mill was dismantled in 1943. In 1946 the revived Empire Redwood company reconstructed the mill and started operations, only to lose the mill by fire in 1947. Rebuilt on a larger scale, this mill was leased to Al Boldt Lumber Co.

Various small mills started operation along the streams between Greenwood Creek and the Gualala river in the 1860's and 1870's such as the Tift and Pound mill, powered by water, at Hardscratch, between Gualala and Point Arena. The largest mill in this area, located on the

FIRST SAWMILL AT FORT BRAGG constructed in 1885 by Fort Bragg Redwood Co. Mill burned in 1888 and was rebuilt when company merged with Noyo Lumber Co. in '91 to form Union Lumber Co. (Photo Union Lumber Co. Collection)

SECOND MILL AT MENDOCINO CITY Built in 1854, mill operated muley saw, two single circular saws with capacity of 60,000 feet a day. (Photo Union Lumber Company Collection)

WILLITS "EXPRESS" READY TO LEAVE FORT BRAGG in 1912. Visitors to redwood coast take train which Union Lumber Company has operated for more than 50 years. Engine was built in 1883, had "57" drivers and weighed 115,000 pounds. (Photo Union Lumber Company Collection)

Garcia river, was completed by Stevens and Whitmore in 1870, and purchased by Byron Nickerson and Samuel Baker in 1872. They operated for almost 20 years, suffering from flood in 1874. Then L. E. White purchased the Garcia mill in 1891, and operated it a few years until the mill burned in 1894. It was not rebuilt.

One of the historic sawmills along the coast began its history when Fred Halmke started a mill late in 1875 at Cuffy Cove. Completed the following year, this mill later became the Redwood Lumber company, which in 1884 was purchased by L. E. White. White rebuilt the mill in 1890 and incorporated in 1894 as the L. E. White Lumber company. He operated successfully for a number of years, cutting the timber in and near the Greenwood Creek basin.

In 1916 the Goodyear Redwood company bought out L. E. White and continued operation until 1930. The Goodyear Redwood company went out of business in 1932. Its mill was operated by the Elk Redwood company in 1934-35. In 1936 this company's portable mill near Elk burned and the large mill at Elk was dismantled, ending a 60-year history of operation near Cuffy Cove. This mill ceased operation because most of its timber was cut.

In 1885 the big production history of the Union Lumber Company began with the operation of the new mill of Fort Bragg Redwood Co. However the actual story started in 1875 at Mill Creek. (Detailed below.)

From 1875 to 1890 various mills were established near Westport, on Wages, De Haven, and Howard creeks. One of the larger of these was the Pollard Lumber company. In 1877 W. R. Miller built a sawmill on Cottoneva Creek near present Rockport. Ten years later this was

taken over by the Cottoneva Lumber company. The Rockport mill burned in 1900. Plans for reconstruction were made, but halted due to difficulties of timber supply.

In 1907 the New York and Pennsylvania Redwood company purchased the property of the Cottoneva Lumber company, also the sawmill and timber of C. A. Hooper on Hardy Creek (originally built in 1895). In 1910 this firm changed its name to Cottoneva Lumber company, and in 1912 its Hardy Creek mill burned. In 1925 the Cottoneva Lumber company sold its property to the Finkbine-Guild company of Mississippi, which completed the long unfinished sawmill in 1926 and started operations. For a short while in 1928 the com-

pany went under the name of Southern Redwood corporation. After 1929 no logs were sawed, and Finkbine-Guild was foreclosed in 1932.

In 1938 Rockport Redwood company took over and resumed operations, until in 1942 its mill burned. The company continued operations by leasing the San Juan Creek sawmill (built in 1939 — burned in 1944) and operating it while rebuilding their Rockport mill. The new mill started operation in 1943, and has been running ever since, with the exception of six months close-down in 1946. Rockport, Union and Caspar were the only major lumber companies which operated on the Mendocino coast during World War II.

UNION'S GREENWOOD CREEK MILL (above) about 1875, later rebuilt by L. E. White. Lumber cars on trucks went down incline to loading chute. (Photo Union Lumber Company Collection)

REDWOOD WATER PIPE used 1885 to 1935. 20-foot logs were bored to 6″ diameter with auger and ends bound with iron hoops which usually rusted before wood rotted. Small ends of pipe were driven into larger and locked with wooden plug. (Photo Union Lumber Company Collection)

Union Lumber company, for more than 50 years the major producer of lumber in Mendocino county, had its origin about 25 years after the first mill was established. In 1875 the Field Bros., built a small sawmill on Mill Creek. This mill burned in 1877, but was rebuilt by the Stewart brothers and Hunter, operating as Newport Sawmill company, in 1878. In 1880 they moved the mill and reconstructed it on the South Fork of Ten Mile river.

Here in 1882, C. R. Johnson arrived and bought a part interest in the firm, which became Stewart, Hunter, and Johnson. In 1884 construction was started on a new sawmill at the site of the old army post known as Fort Bragg, using parts of the Stewart, Hunter, and Johnson

mill. The company was known as the Fort Bragg Redwood company, and C. R. Johnson was its leading figure.

The mill, completed in November, 1885, was destroyed by fire in April 1888 but immediately rebuilt. The Union Lumber company was formed in 1891 by a combination of the Fort Bragg Redwood company, and White and Plummer. The latter company had been cutting principally ties at a sawmill on the Noyo river, originally built by A. W. Macpherson in 1858.

The newly formed Union Lumber company built a tunnel through the ridge between Pudding Creek and the Noyo river to tap the timber in the Noyo basin.

By 1940 the Union Lumber company had become the

SHE CUT REDWOOD FOR 100 YEARS (above) One of last steam mills in California - Caspar L u m b e r Co., 1864-1955. In early operation logs were dropped by spectacular chute from bluff at lower right to Caspar Creek below. (Photo Union Lumber Company Collection)

SAWDUST FOR TENDER GRAPES supplied o u t of 150,000 p o u n d storage of Union Lumber Co. Redwood sawdust was dried in 15 minutes from saw and used for packing grapes for shipment in barrels. (P h o t o Union L u m b e r Company Collection)

leading lumber producer in Mendocino county. In 1905 this company acquired the Little Valley Lumber company mill and timber and part interest in each of the Glen Blair Lumber company and Mendocino Lumber company sawmills and timber holdings.

The earthquake of 1906 did severe damage to Union's sawmill, as it did to many other Mendocino coast mills, because the San Andreas fault, cause of this 'quake, runs along the Mendocino coast. But by June, Union and five other major mills were again running and swamped with orders for lumber for the rebuilding of San Francisco.

The railroad from Fort Bragg to Willits was completed in 1911, allowing lumber shipments to go anywhere in the country by rail, and relieving complete dependence on water shipment. Many surrounding mills came to use the facilities of this railroad, operated by the California Western Railroad and Navigation company, subsidiary of Union Lumber company, and now known as the California Western railroad. For the next 20 years Union Lumber company continued a high rate of production.

A sawmill which had a short life but important bearing on California shipping was the Usal Redwood company, started in 1889 with J. H. Wonderly as president. The sawmill, a 1600 foot wharf, and three miles of railroad had been completed by 1891 at Usal Creek. In 1894 Robert Dollar assumed the management of this company, having run out of timber at his Sonoma county operation. In 1896 Dollar's first steamer "Newsboy" transported lumber from Usal to San Francisco.

During the following year the company was making great strides forward in the lumber business. However, it fell idle by 1902, and shortly after mid-year the sawmill was totally destroyed by fire, which also burned a warehouse, school, and county bridge. The mill was never rebuilt, but Captain Dollar went on to expand his lumber shipping into a general steamship line whose funnel insignia "$" became famous on the Pacific.

In 1901 the Northwestern Redwood company and the Irvine and Muir Lumber company were incorporated. These firms built the first two large redwood mills in the interior of Mendocino county: Northwestern about two miles northwest of Willits and Irvine and Muir at Two Rock Valley. The Northwestern Redwood Lumber company was the first large redwood mill in the county to be able to make regular lumber shipments by rail. In 1903 the Northwestern mill burned, but was immediately rebuilt.

Irvine and Muir built a second mill along the Noyo in 1909, about 14 miles from Willits at a place which came to be known as Irmulco. Operations there ceased about 1912, but in 1916 sawing had been resumed at the mill in Two Rock Valley.

In 1919 some of the Irvine and Muir holdings were sold to Northwestern Redwood company, which had been operating its sawmill fairly steadily for the past 16 years. In 1926 Northwestern Redwood cut its last lumber, and in 1928 its property was taken over by the Irvine-Muir company. However the mill never operated again, and was later dismantled.

Several medium and small sized mills operated both along the coast and in the interior from 1880 to 1930. Some of the older of these include: A. Haun and Sons at Branscomb, whose mill was built in 1884; the Wehrspon mill at Ornbaun, started in 1896; Alpine Lumber company, east of Fort Bragg, starting in 1902; the Glen Blair Lumber company near Fort Bragg, organized in 1903 from the Pudding Creek lumber (started in 1888); and Ukiah Redwood Lumber company, Ukiah. There were other mills in Anderson Valley, near Ukiah, Willits,

Laytonville, and the vicinities of Potter Valley and Covelo.

The Southern Humboldt Lumber company in 1904 was building a new mill at Andersonia (now Piercy) on the South Fork of the Eel river. A railroad was also under construction up Indian Creek through the low gap near Kenney and over to Bear Harbor. A large volume of logs was cut to supply the new mill. Then in 1905, as the sawmill was about to start, its owner, Henry Anderson, was hit by one of the first logs being hauled to the mill. He died, and this mill never operated.

By 1947 his grandsons had recovered the property, formed the Indian Creek Lumber company, and rebuilt the mill on the old site. The first logs cut were those which had lain around the mill for 42 years. Others had been lying in the woods during that time. About 15 per cent recovery was obtained and 400,000 board feet salvaged. This mill later changed its name to Andersonia Lumber company, and in 1953 was under lease to T. M. Dimmick company.

Before and during World War II, several of the now larger mills in the county started operation in a small way. Ben Mast's sawmill, 4 miles west of Laytonville, started operations in 1937. McDougall Lumber company started operations near Branscomb in 1941 with a sawmill moved over from Lake county. This mill went through several ownerships, in 1949 becoming the Wilson-Beedy Lumber company, which boosted its production into the large mill class. Within the past year this mill has been taken over by Vernie Jack, former mill superintendent for Wilson-Beedy.

The Ukiah Pine Lumber company commenced operation in 1942, at Van Arsdale Reservoir, part of which is used as a log pond. The Saga Land and Improvement company sawmill at Willits was completed early in 1943

LOADING REDWOOD ON FREIGHTER by cable and carriage off Noyo River near Fort Bragg. C. R. Johnson (Union Lumber Co.) and associates operated National Steamship Co. building and buying many vessels, such as **Noyo, National City, Brunswick, Coquille River, South Coast, Higgins, Berkeley, Fort Bragg** and **Phoenix**. (Photo Union Lumber Co. Collection)

largely from materials and equipment moved over from the idle Glen Blair mill site. It operated only 2½ years until destroyed by fire in mid-1945. However, this mill was a forerunner of Willits Redwood Products company.

From 1945 to 1948 sawmills built include that of W. C. Thompson operated by the Crawford Lumber Company; Harold Casteel mill at Willits which burned in 1946 and was rebuilt by Pacific Coast Company; Hollow Tree Lumber Company near Hale's Grove which mill was sold to D. M. W. Lumber Company. Hollow Tree then took over a mill near Ukiah; Jensen Lumber Company Willits, later sold to Little Lake Lumber Company, Ukiah Lumber Mills Inc. whose mill north of that city was completed in 1947 and sold to Stoll Lumber Company. From 1950 to 1953 new mills were completed by Wolf Creek Lumber Company at Jackass Creek, Coombs Lumber Company south of Piercy, Ridgewood Lumber Company at Willits; H. E. Casteel Industries north of Ukiah, Aborigine Lumber Company near Fort Bragg, Mendocino Wood Products Company at the Ridgewood Ranch.

THE COOKHOUSE IS GONE

"Ulysses S. Grant had just died, there were only thirty-eight states in the Union, Grover Cleveland was serving his first term as president — and in the redwoods C. R. Johnson was completing his new sawmill." This is the way Alder Thurman set the pace for his account of the Union Lumber Company's old cookhouse in the company's house organ — The Noyo Chief.

"An early entry in the Journal and Cash Book on May 19, 1885, showed 'provisions and dishes for the cookhouse, $82.07.' The dishes were a far cry from English china, but the food they held was no respecter of elegant service. The only requirement being that the platters were big enough and that there were plenty of them.

"There was an overseer or manager, six Chinese cooks, two or three local women or boys to serve, and a bullcook for making the beds and cleaning the rooms. Twenty-three bunk rooms were on the second floor of the cookhouse for the 'board and roomers.' There the single men lived and the married ones who had left their wives elsewhere. Many of the married men later sent for their families and established a home up town. As the single boys married, others moved in to take their places. There was always a long waiting list. The food was good and $15 a month in the '90's brought them three man-filling meals every 24 hours. In addition to the regular roomers, most of the Plant workers ate at least one or more meals a day at the cookhouse.

WHERE AH JIM COOKED FOR SAWMILL CREWS. Famous cookhouse at C. R. Johnson's new mill in Mendocino County, California, built in 1885. For $15 a month a man got everything from mush to mulligan three times a day and a room on the second floor. One of the Chinese cooks was Young Chan, later a Fort Bragg merchant. (Photo Union Lumber Company Collection)

"The big dining room with its long, oil cloth-covered tables, could hold up to 120 men at one serving. The tables had benches seating four on each side. A coffee pot and a tea pot were permanent fixtures on every table. The huge ranges were wood fed, their ovens turning out the white beans and yellow cake that never missed a meal.

"The bill of fare consisted of eggs, mush, hotcakes, mulligan stews, fried steaks, corned beef and cabbage, sowbelly, spuds, hash, roast chicken, pies, puddings, the afore-mentioned white beans and yellow cake and more — all piled skyward on the bulky, white glazed pottery platters. No one went away hungry and second and third helpings were expected.

"The Mill worked two 10-hour shifts, from 7 to 6 and 7 to 6. Meals were served every six hours at 6 and 12 and 6 and 12. The four meals a day kept the cooks hopping and often hopping mad. More than one of the gay young blades who tried to sneak in the kitchen ahead of time for a between-meals' snack was sent running by a sharper blade on the end of a wicked looking meat cleaver held aloft by a swearing, sputtering Chinese cook.

"In the early '20's the midnight meal was 'on the house.' It was the forerunner of the night shift bonus. For many years the foreman's Friday lunches were looked

AND THEY WERE SIX FOOTERS Largest board cut in Humboldt County at the time — 3"x81"x18' — displayed by four gay blades of Hammond Lumber Company in 1890. (Photo courtesy Hammond - California Redwood Company)

forward to from week to week. They were an opportunity for getting together to talk over work methods and production schedules.

"In the days before the movie houses, radios and such, the evenings were spent in the combination recreation and library room. Over 200 books were available for the literary minded. A commissary where candy and tobacco were sold was open every noon and for three hours in the evening. Many a friendly argument which began as an exchange of words soon became an exchange of strength. A set of boxing gloves was handy in the recreation room to make might the master of right, but in a more gentlemanly method than bare fists.

"In the early days, the Company paid in gold and silver. Card games, a favorite form of recreation wherever men gathered, were always to be found in the evenings and on pay days the poker games took over. Often as much as $500 winnings (a very tidy sum in those days) would be gathered in an all-night session.

"No doubt many of the men working for the Company today learned much about life as 'small frys' sitting in on the worldly and unworldly bull sessions held on the cookhouse steps. For, in spite of the 10-hour shifts, there was more leisure time than now and many hours were spent by the wood-whittling philosophers on the cookhouse veranda. And many were the tales told by the sea captains and sailors, off the lumber schooners tied up at the wharf, that filled the young fellows with dreams of adventures and life on the high seas.

"Times change and the world about us moves on. As the years rolled by, the character of the lumberjack and the mill worker changed, too. The old-timers moved on to make way for their sons and their sons' sons. This younger generation, now settled in the community was a stable group. They married, built homes, became active in community life and took their places in the Woods and Plant. Fewer jobs were taken by single fellows from outside of the area and in January of 1951 an era passed. The cook house closed its doors for all time.

"In late 1952 the building was torn down. The lumber and fixtures were sold, the old hand-made, square nails were exclaimed over and the ashes from the few remaining wood scraps were watered down and hauled away to be returned to the dust from which they had come centuries before as small, redwood seedlings.

"Although any story of a building where men have lived, laughed and sometimes shed a tear, is also a story of their individual personalities, it is far more the story of an atmosphere created by their total, accumulated thoughts and actions. It is for this reason and the fact that many names must of necessity by the falling away of contacts be not easily recollected by those still here that individuals have not been named throughout this article. They all contributed their bit to this passing panorama and some whose names are fresher in the minds of people relating background for this article are these.

"Mrs. Sydney Williams, Guy Weller's mother-in-law, was one of the first cookhouse managers. W. W. Ware, O. H. Seaholm and Fred Hervilla took their turns at running things. There was C. G. Hing, who hired the Chinese cooks and helpers; Young Chan, now a retired Fort Bragg merchant, was a cook. Frank Thompson ran the commissary for years. Mrs. Norberry and her daughter, Hazel, waited on tables. There were these and many more.

"The cookhouse building is gone, but the cookhouse memories will always remain to quicken the pulse and fill the air with warm nostalgia wherever former 'room and boarders' gather to reminisce."

SCOTIA BEFORE FIRE which in 1895 destroyed most of mill and all stacked lumber. (Photo courtesy Pacific Lumber Company)

MARVELOUS ONE-MAN SAWMILL

It wasn't until last summer that we discovered the one and only sawmill we have ever seen that had the labor problem solved. This mill, not very far from Bend, has had the same crew for five years steady, not a man has quit nor has a man been added to the payroll in all that time. It is a modern outfit, in that it has some machinery consisting of several cogwheels, chains, levers and a 1910 model Chevrolet engine in it. The man that built the mill is also the owner of it. He is, too, the chief engineer, fireman, head grader and crew. In fact, it is a one-man sawmill.

We came across this contraption hidden in the woods not far from the road, being attracted to it by the coughing sound given out by the engine, which seemed to be having some kind of trouble with its respiratory organs. At first sight we took it to be a moonshine still, but we promptly discarded that idea as nobody shot at us when we hove in view. Then our startled eye took in a heterogeneous mess of sprockets, monkey wrenches, peavies and flywheels and we knew we had discovered something even more interesting than a still, if there is anything more interesting than a still.

The owner was engaged in the brain racking job of siwashing a log onto the home-made carriage with a peavy, and inasmuch as whenever he got one end on the other fell off, his attention was occupied for the moment, so we leaned carefully up against a roof support to watch the proceedings. Each time he slammed his end of the log against the blocks the mill shook from stem to stern

and threatened to collapse in eleven different places. He finally succeeded in getting one end under a log, but just as he was about to lift the other back on the carriage he had to stop and run around the headrig to jiggle a little piece of bailing wire which did something to the carburetor. The engine having taken on new life and slid into its customary idling speed of somewhere around 90 miles an hour, he returned to his deck job, talking loudly to himself. He had to talk loud to hear himself above the power plant, but it was easy to see that he was an educated man. His language was composed of the finest collection of cuss words it has ever been our pleasure to hear and we've been around sawmills for 20 years. He was a walking Thesaurus of real old lumberjack swear words, and he used the most terrifying language without showing the least sign of being mad at anything.

After getting the log safely fastened on the carriage and the dogs hammered home, the old fellow dodged nimbly around to the sawyer's cage and had a talk with himself in which he discovered that the engineer was out of gasoline. He stopped the carriage mechanism by taking a stick and knocking a couple of belts off the wheels. He jiggled the carburetor in exactly the same manner that he used to keep it going, as far as we were able to see, but this time the engine stopped. When the engine, with its accompanying assortment of belts, wheels, waffle irons and whatnot, had stopped going around, the silence was deafening, but the owner kept right on talking just as loud as ever.

"—hev tew put another leetle touch o' grease on them thar tracks purty soon," he yelled to himself as

FIRST AT FORESTVILLE Early Pacific Lumber Co. mill at what is now Scotia, California, which gave company its early start in one of the biggest redwood operations. (Photo courtesy Pacific Lumber Company)

the noise subsided. "Seems ez how they squeak a mite more'n usual t'day."

Dexterously slipping half a gill of snuff under his lip, he replaced a sprocket which had shaken itself loose from its moorings, tightened up three nuts and emptied an oil can on a flywheel bearing, after which he picked up an empty coal oil can and retired to a shack in the rear where he filled up with gasoline. He refilled the tank over his engine, gave the crank a twist and with half a dozen backfires which threatened to blow the engine off its foundation, the machinery got under way again. Two or three boards rattled off the roof and part of the back wall swayed six inches with each convulsion, but the building managed to hang together. The general manager of the plant cocked a speculative eye at the hole in the roof where the boards had been and sized up the weather through a place where a wall had once stood.

"Wal, I'll be blinkety blank blanked," he bellowed conversationally, grinning amiably at us as we clung desperately to a post to keep from being shaken off the deck. "Thet makes three times them thar blink blank boards has shook off the blank blank roof this summer. It don't make no differ'nce though. We don't git much rain in this blankety blink blink country."

The carriage, rolling on four wooden spools, wobbled down a track made of 2x4's on edge. As the wheels were a couple of inches too wide for the track there was a slight variation in the cut of from a half an inch to two inches, depending on how far the carriage sagged as it went past the saw, and a grade inspector would have had difficulty in classifying some of the boards. They started through on an inch cut, but it was nothing out of the ordinary to have the board come out 8x4 on one end and drop siding on the other. Every time a slab fell onto the deck something come loose in the mill and it felt as if an earthquake had just passed under us. The carriage was pulled back and forth by means of a rope passed over a wooden drum at each end of the deck, and the engineer ran it with some kind of a clutch arrangement of wooden blocks. The clutch slipped several seconds before it took hold, and when it did get all braced to pull the carriage back the rope stretched out a couple of feet before anything moved and the result was more or less nerve racking. We got a fresh hold on our post, braced our feet and gritted our teeth prepared for the shock we knew was going to hit us when the contraption moved, but as it was thirty seconds—a half minute completely filled with groans, squeaks and backfires from the engine—before the machinery actually got into action one was always taken off guard when the carriage began

SCOTIA WITH MILL RE-BUILT after disastrous 1895 fire. (Photo courtesy Pacific Lumber Company)

to move.

Whenever it was time to turn the log the proprietor of the outfit kicked off a couple of belts, poured a little water on the clutch, tightened up all the nuts and bolts that had come loose during the past ten minutes, seized his peavy, went around on the other side of the carriage and pried the log over, after knocking the dogs loose with a hammer. When it came to rest in a position that looked as if it might ride through the saw once or twice without falling off, he reversed the process by crawling back over the log, tightening half a dozen nuts that he had missed the first time, pouring a little more water on the still smoking clutch and putting all the belts back on. There was nothing steady or sure about this routine, however, as he was constantly obliged to drop everything from time to time while he rushed over and jiggled the carburetor wire.

"Got tew rig me up a blink blink extension on thet blankety blank blink wire some o' these days," he roared, as he gave the flywheel another squirt of oil for good luck. "She keeps slowin' down on me."

The engine itself was worthy of close study. He didn't have to put oil in it because there were no two pieces that rubbed together any place. It had a miscellaneous collection of petcocks, gauges, tin cans or what-have-you hung around on it and a half a mile of barbed wire fence supplemented the base bolts in holding it down. When the slack had finally all been taken out of the belts, sprockets, clutch and rope and the engine was working real hard, it stood itself on end and shook sideways like a crab, but it never did stop. It had a dirty habit of throwing set-screws, spark plugs and main springs at the boss whenever he came too close to it and every now and then the flywheel fell off and rolled out through a hole in the wall. The only good thing about it seemed to be that it always rolled the same way.

"She bust that blinkety blank blank hole in th' wall more'n two years ago," screamed the general manager

in a satisfied way, "an' she ain't missed th' blink blink thing sence."

The circular saw blade which whittled its way through the log in a snaky and meandering manner, something like the trail left by poor old Uncle Tom while trying to dodge the bloodhounds, had been set back in '25 by a traveling tinner, and it needed a few new teeth here and there. A saw to this owner was just a piece of iron with some rough spots on it, and he couldn't be bothered. He bought all his parts from an auto wrecking plant in the city and there were so many substitute parts hung around on things that you'd have thought it was a drug store. If the junk shops ever went out of business the mill would have had to shut down automatically.

Whenever he had piled up eight or ten boards and wrestled another log onto the carriage he held a conference with himself and found out that it was time for the engineer to jiggle the wire again. That little job attended to it was necessary for the millwright to climb under the rig and see why it was that the carriage went ahead when he pulled the reverse lever, and vice versa. Having done this he put on his fireman's hat and dashed over to the water pail to put out the fire in the clutch. At five o'clock he blew a whistle to tell himself when to quit and then tallied up the day's cut. If it was a good day he sometimes had as much as 600 feet ready for edging.

But he had no labor trouble. The mill ran every day as regular as clock work and he didn't have to fire a man and then go out looking for someone to take his place. There were no orders up on the boards along Portland's slave market calling for men for this outfit. And from all appearances the owner was just a little more satisfied and at peace with the world than any sawmill owner we have ever met. We'd like to have one of these one-man outfits ourself if it wasn't such hard work.

. . . from Brooks-Scanlon Deschutes Pine Echoes

130

CLEARS *and* STARS

THE SHINGLE MACHINE

"Zing, zim; zing, zim," sings the machine,
  The shingle machine.
And the thin saws croon,
  "Soon, soon, sawyer-man,
  We'll sing you to sleep, and leap
  At your blind, dumb hand.
  Sawyer-man, as you stand
  Serving us long,
  Mind our song
  When we croon 'Soon, soon'."
               . . . Charles Oluf Olsen

"All right," the public of the 1880s said, "we've got boards for walls and floors but we can't keep on using mud, sod and stone for roofs. Give us something thin, light and strong that will shed rain and snow and last a long time." And what the public got was the cedar shingle.

This piece of home building merchandise delivered such good value, the business of cutting it mushroomed into a major industry in the Pacific Northwest in three decades. It started in the early '80s along the Columbia River with little hand machine mills hanging on the edge of the wet cedar forests. And by the time the Northern Pacific railroad came to the Coast and shingle making machinery had been introduced, mills were really in business.

In 1893 there were 150 of them shipping shingles to the Middle West by rail and out of the Columbia and Puget Sound by schooner. Bolts were $2.50 a cord at the mill which by hand method, employing 7 or 8 men and cutting one block at a time, turned out 30 to 50 thousand feet a day. Many of these little mills were powered by waterwheels up to 1900 and even later. Shingles were dried over steam coils. And most of the men came from Wisconsin and Michigan.

The larger mills, using single and double block as well as 10-block machines, did better. They worked about 25 men and packed 125 to 140 M a day. These mills had steam power, some of them electric light plants, dryhouses, oil houses and warehouses. And they were selling shingles in 1902 for $2 a thousand loaded on railway cars.

G. A. ONN SHINGLE MILL AT DRYAD was typical of the many small plants in the timber-rich Chehalis River area on the South Bend branch. A hot-tempered taskmaster, Onn fired the entire crew several times and son Harry was forced to round them up and rehire them before they wandered off to the next mill. (Photo courtesy H. B. Onn)

BOLT TRAIN Narrow gauge, saddle-tank lokey of Independent Coal and Coke Co. with sled loads of shingle bolts loaded on flat cars. (Darius Kinsey photo from Jesse E. Ebert Collection)

By 1895 2 million feet of cedar shingles a day came out of 40 Whatcom County, Wash., mills alone with Skagit producing about the same, and the Chehalis River-Grays Harbor area bringing up third. Early mills were Howard and Attick at Edison which ferried its shingles across Puget Sound to schooners at Port Blakely; Col. P. A. Woolley and his sons operating the Skagit River Lumber and Shingle Co. which had already begun to cut cedar siding; Sparks and Monaghan at Getchell — all in the Skagit area.

In Bellingham, D. H. DeCan built the first shingle mill on the tide flats bay at the foot of F Street. It was a hand machine mill with the Riddle brothers as knot sawyers. In 1904, S. H. Siemens and son built a 10-block mill at the mouth of Squalicum Creek and at this time the Loggie mill with two 10-block machines was the country's biggest producer. In 1890 the Fleming and Earles mill at Fairhaven was operating two 10-block machines.

Shingle bolts were cut 52" in the woods, 20 to 40 bolts to the cord. They were skidded by horses and sleds directly to mills or dumped in rivers and floated down the mills' fin booms. Some mills not on rivers used flumes to get the bolts in.

Cut off saws divided the bolts into 16", 18" and 24" lengths. These blocks dropped to belts or carriages which brought them up against smaller, quartering saws which cut across the diameter, turned them and cut at right angles to the first cut. This gave blocks proper size for handling and opened the grain for cutting vertical or edgegrain shingles.

Blocks then went to a third saw which trimmed off bark and surface defects, then up a conveyor to the second floor and shingle machines. Blocks were placed in machines so saws cut against the face, blocks shifting backward and forward, the top extending farther than the bottom on one forward movement and reversely on the next movement, the wedge shape being produced.

As shingles came from machine, knot sawyers squared up edges and trimmed out defects, throwing them down chutes to bins on floor below. Defective shingles were kept separate.

Packers made up bundles of standard size, bunching them in a hand machine or "packer," and binding bun-

PRIDE OF BURPEE Clipper Shingle Factory in Burpee, Washington Territory, owned by E. P. Marsh. Ray Moore who filed in many of Washington's early shingle mills, recalls the most popular place in Burpee was the Wink Eye Saloon. (Photo courtesy Ray Moore)

dles with thin iron straps and strips of hemlock. Conveyor belts took bundles to dry kilns where they took the steam heat treatment for ten days to two weeks, a slow method to keep shingles from splitting. By this time the wood had contracted and the bundles had to be retied.

"Everett — The Shingle Capital Of The World," said the Great Northern Railway in 1915 and the old shingle weavers do not deny it. It was a city of smoke stacks and labor trouble with the shingle men highly paid aristocrats. Ray Moore, a 42-year veteran of the cedar mills, remembers Everett's heyday when he landed there, a raw kid from Saginaw. Clough and Hartley's was the largest siding and shingle mill in the world, they said. And there were dozens more — Canyon Lumber Co., Ferry-Baker, Eclipse, Seaside, Northwest, Everett-Best, Super Shingle Co. In Marysville were the Alki and Dickinson Shingle Co. At Milltown, W. J. Henry and Holly's "White Elephant" mill.

"Sure was lucky I had that money hid in my school books," said Ray Moore, whose Everett saw shop is the headquarters for shingle weavers of five Washington counties. "I just grabbed it and ran. Left New Year's day, I remember. My father was foreman and filed for Arthur Rhodes shingle mill at Leota, Michigan, but I wanted the big wide West. My money got me to Minneapolis and a couple of 'real pals' got me a scalper's train ticket to Everett. Man — that Everett was a big place. I was 17 with a cattail in each ear. Got off in the railroad yards — no friends, no place to go, no money. Only half a loaf of bread to eat all that time on the train. Well I did have 7¢ and spent 5 of it for a sack of Bull Durham. Then I spotted a big nail factory — the Puget Sound Wire Nail and Steel Co. — and a boarding house kitchen. There was a big stack of dishes and I asked the lady — 'Can I wash them for supper and a room?'

I told her I was a shingle weaver which I wasn't and she told me about the big Eclipse mill. In the morning I wandered that way, into the mill and watched a 10-block machine work. Then suddenly a big ball of wet sawdust hit me in the back of the neck and I grabbed a stick and started after the grinning ape, smacking him on the top of the head. Well then it got serious and he was after me. I dodged through the first door I saw.

HE RAN AWAY FROM SAGINAW at 17 and lived the life of a shingle weaver "up, down and sideways." Ray Moore packed a long life into his early days, still works at his saw shop in Everett, headquarters for shingle men of five counties. He remembers the "Everett Massacre," Billy Gohl and a mule that saved his life. (Photo Ray Moore Collection)

Man, oh man! Believe it or not, I heard a voice out of somewhere — 'Ray, what are you doin' 'way out here?' Then the man I hit was on me — but off quick like. Because there was Del Woodward who had worked with my father in those Michigan shingle mills most of his life. He jumped on the guy and threatened him. 'Don't you ever touch that kid!' He didn't — just grinned some more and left. Nobody else ever went after those cattails in this green kid any more. For my timely found friend was the filer and he had authority. 'You're goin' to work, Ray. Most of the men around here are from Saginaw and around.' So I did — knot sawing at $5 a day. Yessir, that's where I learned about trimming, edging and squaring clears and stars. Stayed a year and a half. Went back home to level things with my father. Then back to the Coast, installing shingle machinery."

Ray Moore knew all the old characters in the mills around Everett and later in Aberdeen and Vancouver, B.C. There was Bill Legole, shingle sawyer who set the world's hand machine record and did his own filing.

There was Paddy Young who looked for a job 15 years and finally turned the work over to his squaw. He came back to Everett for his mail about once in two years. Ray knew the rough-and-tough fighters of the day — Bugs Crisp, Streeter, Billy Ross who took the shingle mill championship away from Si Gotchy. And the gamblers who blew up the safe in Everett's Industrial Loan Company office.

The shingle mills, large and small, were booming everywhere north of the Columbia. Along the rain-soaked valleys of the Lewis River, the Snoqualmie, Chehalis, Nooksack and Elwha there were little mills every ten miles and every one a man or two short of enough. Mammoth operations like the Clear Lake Lumber Co. were filling up freight cars and ships at the rate of 100 and 200 thousand feet a day. Brattlie Bros. mill in Ridgefield was going great guns and Brattlie-trained sawyers and filers were fanning out to work at other mills and start their own.

Harry B. Onn of Dryad and Doty, Washington, has a story about those days too. "My father **had** bought the

EARLY SHINGLE MILL NEAR STANWOOD. (Photo Darius Kinsey courtesy Bernard Lawe)

old Vaughan and Hayes mill in 1894 and renamed it the
G. A. Onn Shingle Co. He had been a blacksmith and
carriage builder as well as mayor in Montgomery, Minnesota, and later owned a railroad hotel in Minneapolis.
When he sold that in 1886, he headed for Tacoma. The
rest of us — mother, my older brother George and myself — followed the next year. We traveled west on an
old-fashioned immigrant train with a big cookstove in
the end of every car and seats were let down to make
beds. Everybody carried his own bedding. The cars had
open vestibules at the ends and us kids played in them
and on the railings. It's sure a wonder half of us weren't
lost overboard. We had no trouble with Indians except
fighting them off at every depot in North Dakota and
Montana. Those Mandans and Blackfeet were all over
you trying to sell souvenirs, mostly hatracks made from
pairs of polished buffalo horns.

"When dad bought the mill George and I worked in
it and later I was bookkeeper. Mother ran the cookhouse — and a job that was, too. There were 18 or 20
homesteaders on claims up Elk Creek who came down
pack trails to get supplies at Dryad and always managed
to make the cookhouse in time for the midday meal. If
they had two-bits that was o.k. If they didn't, they were

welcome just the same. None of them ever went home
hungry. They all had warm spots in their hearts, like
the fellows in the mill, for Mother Onn and her cooking.

"Dryad was a lively little burg in those days. Mill
owners and operators were J. A. Dennis, G. A. Onn,
Chandler Brothers, Schlenar and Hauser, Leudinghouse
Brothers with a 10-block machine and another plant with
hand machine and upright and Wasser Brothers with
four uprights.

"The Northern Pacific had built a line to Raymond
and South Bend in 1892 and commemorated the occasion
by running a special train for Frederick W. Weyerhaeuser. They frequently ran trains of 100 cars east but
the ways and means of handling cargo was sometimes
kind of crude. There was no siding at Dryad and once
when a flat car of machinery and goods was billed here
the train stayed until as many hands as could be drafted,
including passengers, were put to work unloading it."

Onn, senior, Harry recalls, was a rugged individualist
with a two-fisted temper. "Mill crews were hard to manage in those days because men could quit for any or no
reason, walk to the next mill in a day or less and go
right to work. Dad had a hard time holding himself in
and several times blew the lid clear off and fired the

SHINGLE MILL FED BY THREE-MILE FLUME
Shingle and planing mill in Washington's Skagit River area in 1913 at terminus of flume. (All Darius Kinsey photos from Jesse E. Ebert Collection)

whole crew. Being bookkeeper in charge of the payroll, I had the measley job of rounding them all up and getting them to go to work again.

"Another time while fixing the stove pipe in the old boarding house, he let his temper fly and the cast iron contraption which was held together by four iron rods, collapsed. Piece by piece he carried it outside and threw everything down the river bank. That night, just before dark, we saw him retrieving the pieces. In the morning that stove was fired up doing its job as good as ever.

"In those days shingle mills and saloons seemed to go hand in hand. In Dryad the shingle weavers could quench their thirsts or drown their sorrows at Al Flood's,

Wakefield and McCracken's, C. C. Bowers', Speaker and Brossard's and Bowers and Brown's. These places were open 24 hours a day with wide open gambling and people seemed to have plenty of money. There weren't any cars and gas and movies."

And Harry Onn recalls the famous Dark Day when smoke and ashes of the big forest fire blacked out the countryside for a hundred miles around. "What did people do? All the men got drunk and the women either cried or prayed, some of them both. I thought there was something wrong with our clock so I lighted the kerosene lantern and took off for the shingle mill. The only person there was little Tom Howell. He and I went up

ANCIENT MARINER POLES BOLTS from Skagit River (below) into flume conveyor. (Center) 40-foot flume followed mountain stream three miles to mill. (Right) 1,100 shingle bolts in pond at mill.

2400 CORDS OF SHINGLE BOLTS in 1924 at booming ground of Hastings Shingle Manufacturing Co. mill near Rainy River, Howe Sound, B.C. (Photo courtesy British Columbia Forest Service)

town. You fill in the rest.

"Were the men pretty tough and strong? Guess they had to be. I remember Big Pete Thompson stealing one of Charley Mauermann's calves and carrying it across the N.P. bridge under his arm and up in the mill bunkhouse. He probably wondered why he did it but set the calf down on the floor and went to bed. It took G. A. Onn and several other men to get the animal back down on the ground. And at one 4th of July celebration, Bill Ludwig walked a tight-rope over the Chehalis River with a keg of beer on his head. Mike Madden was the speaker of the day and as a sideline was supposed to go over the Loudinghouse dam in a washtub. And Andy

Hilburger was going to dive into the river from the top of the railroad bridge. Do I have to remember whether they did or not?"

Chris C. Seigal, writing in the Shingle Weaver, upon the death of James L. Pinkey, said great rivalry existed among the early day shingle men. "In 1902 Jim Pinkey cut 136½ thousand shingles in a 10-hour shift. This record was accomplished at the Parker Bros. Shingle Mill of Lawrence. A thousand shingles consisted of four bunches shingles are measured by squares containing 24 courses each. Today with four bunches containing 20 courses, which is a square of 800 shingles. Had shingles been measured in squares 54 years ago, Pinkey's

cut would have been more than 160 squares.

"Shingle weavers in those early days consisted of saw filers, sawyers, knee bolters, knot sawyers and packers. Other workers in the mills were just laborers. There was considerable rivalry among the various crafts as to who was the champion in his branch of the industry. No one ever came close to Jim Pinkey's cut. Gus Larson was a runner up but was less than 100 thousand.

"In 1905 a young man named Clyde Harrison, 22, packed 84 thousand shingles at Lytells Shingle Mill at Hoquiam in a 10-hour shift. This record has never been equalled. Harrison died in Kelso two years ago at the age of 73.

"In 1904 Jack Horn, a knot sawyer at the Manley and Sons Mill at Lake Samish, set up a record for knot sawing by handling 56 thousand shingles in 10 hours

SLED TRAIN hauled by early Caterpillar crawler tractor. (Darius Kinsey photo from Jesse E. Ebert Collection)

BLAINE SHINGLE WEAVERS Crew of Newcomb Shingle Mill, Blaine, Wash., takes time out to pose with Clears, Stars and Kinsey photographs. (Darius Kinsey photo from Jesse E. Ebert)

SHINGLE BOLT LOADING RIG in 1925 driven by gasoline engine. Chain belt picked up bolts from pond, dumped them in crib. (Photo courtesy British Columbia Forest Service)

out of raw timber. Raw timber was split blocks, not knee bolted. This was an ordinary days work for two knot sawyers. Jack died a number of years ago in Everett.

"The old time shingle weavers had a disastrous general strike in 1906, which nearly wrecked the union. The union was poorly organized with less than 50 per cent of the active weavers as members. A man from Bay City, Mich., was president and was not familiar with local conditions. A strike was called at the Simpson Mill Co. at Ballard but the mill company had little difficulty in securing a crew. As a result, Bolger, the union president, came out from Michigan and at a conference of local unions, a general strike was ordered.

"In May, 1906, the union members were called out. The union was so poorly organized that the strike became a dismal failure and in less than three months all the weavers were back on the job with no gains from the strike."

From men like Eli Buckley who worked almost 60 years in Washington and British Columbia shingle mills, Gerald Massie, filer at Jamison's in Everett, from Charley

White at Ridgefield, E. E. Boyd at Acme and Ray Thompson of the "Shingle Weaver," come colorful yarns of the old days when men of the Northwest woods thought they would never see the end of the cedar. And the names they had —

Michigan Slim Allen, upright sawyer; Can Kelly, short staker; Shoepac Johnson; Whisky Martin; Balky Bill Amsbury, hand machine sawyer; Whistling Rufus (Peo Bessemer), upright sawyer; Music Box Charlie; Workhouse Johnson; Chalky Dennis; Peanuts (Gaston Laviolette) packer; Froggy Berg; Gooseneck Clampitt, knot sawyer; Skabanga (John Napolean) kneebolter; Twostep Peterson, packer; Snifty Pete Godderz, Hall machine sawyer; Old Rippy — Billy Ried, packer; Old Barbee — Walter Hammons, knot sawyer and upright sawyer; Vinegar Bill Ferrier, double-block sawyer and filer; Stuttering Andy Stevenson, packer.

Add the Chinamen in the Hastings and Canada Shingle Co. mills in Vancouver, B.C. Ray Moore remembers they all went around with their sing-song — " 'It no rain no mol — no mol!' I used to call 'em all Charlie and ask 'em why they didn't quit. 'No quit. Get bellyache'."

SUNDAY IN SHINGLE LAND Wobbly-kneed guzzler hoists another beer in front of Pilchuck saloon as customers try to stand still. Bartender on chair is only one smiling. Note planked sidewalk and street. (Photo courtesy Ray Moore)

THE INFLUENCE OF SWEDISH BREAKFAST FOOD ON THE LUMBER INDUSTRY
by PAUL HOSMER
Reprinted from Brooks-Scanlon "Pine Echoes"

Not long ago the editor of the New Yorker, a most estimable publication, stubbed his toe on something on the sidewalk and investigation disclosed that he had tripped over an empty snuff box. A short time before there had been a shooting affray on this particular spot and the editor immediately jumped to the conclusion that a couple of old southern gallants had been fighting a duel.

The editor, being an investigator of the highest type and a very observing person, was much surprised to discover that snuff was still being used in this country and the fact started him off on the trail of what he thought was a good story. He interviewed a corner tobacconist and found that while there once had been a snuff making plant in Helmeta, New Jersey, founded in 1760, the plant had been abandoned and had been taken over by the city to be preserved as a memorial. The tobacconist also informed the editor, in his knowing way, that snuff was still being used by a few people in the south and middle West and also by a few Norwegian sailors and some New England salts along the Atlantic coast. He was surprised, however, to learn from the tobacco man that few people sniff the stuff, most of them now merely placing a pinch of the concoction between cheek and gum and apparently remaining content to leave it there quietly and unostentatiously while nature pursues the even tenor of its ways. He was also much surprised to learn that some people even chew it.

Further investigation on the part of the editor brought to light the fact that although snuff is carried in one Fifth Ave. shop in three different flavors, it is seldom

140

called for. The editor concluded that ladies who "manipulated jewelled snuff-boxes to show their diamond rings, handsome hands and snowy arms," now reach for a sweetie instead of a Lucky, or something.

We have no doubt that if the editor of the New Yorker ever read a Pine Echoes — which he probably never will — he would immediately catalog us as too provincial for words, which is all right with us. We're not a bit proud. But in our humble way we can't help but feel that the editor of the New Yorker is not so hot himself when it comes to knowing the world outside of New York. Is it possible there is a man in America who doesn't realize the important part snuff plays in present day affairs? God only knows how many thousands of words we've written about snuff in the past few years, but alas, it

SAWYER TURNED SCRAPPER Si Gotchy (left) was an Everett shingle weaver who saw easier money in the ring. Heading out of Stevens Point, Wisc., he became pile driver, heavy construction worker, shingle sawyer and finally Olympia, Wash., police officer. On the back of this photograph he wrote: "I sawed ten hours the day of this fight with Bugs Crisp (in Montesano, 1918) and it was a draw. Beat him later in Elma. The guy behind me on the left is Frank Stone who was mixed up with Jack Gillis looting the Industrial Insurance Fund of nearly $100,000. Lee Williams, the Montana Kid, is behind my head. The guy in between Bugs and me is Casey Jones, Tacoma fighter who got sent up later for robbery. The others are bartenders, pimps and gambler. Would you think a shingle weaver would keep this kind of company? They were all good guys except me." Photo courtesy Ray Moore)

REED AND FREEMAN operated this shingle mill in 1899 at site where Pictsweet plant now stands. Jack Reed had been filer at Clear Lake shingle mill and Freeman also made shingles with J. C. Waugh. Fin boom extended out into Skagit River to catch cedar bolts logged as far up as Lyman and sheer boom brought them to mill. John Wylie also hauled bolts out of woods and recalls mill had a box kiln with no outside valve to turn off steam. "They burned the shingles up drying them to 225 pounds a thousand to beat freight rates East. You also burned yourself up getting in to turn that steam off." (Photo courtesy John Wylie)

GRAYS HARBOR SHINGLE MILL Interior of Aloha Lumber Co. mill at Aloha, Washington. Logs were sawed, cut into blocks and passed to equalizer at right. (Photo University of Washington)

has been for nought. The editor of the New Yorker hasn't heard a word of it, and an empty snuff box starts him off on an ineffectual scoop of his own. If he had ever set foot outside of New York and had suffered himself to be led astray by every discarded snuff can he ran across he would have found himself in a state closely bordering on epilepsy in the first couple of hours.

From what we can pick up about it, a party by the name of Lief Erickson was the first man to come to America. Lief is the person who got off the first good Swede joke. It seems that when he got home and his first son was born his wife caught him in his night shirt picking up the baby about midnight one night. "What are you doing?" she asked. "Oh, Aye yust ban turning over a new Lief," replied Mr. Erickson, and that was that. Anyway, Lief wandered over into America in some way or other and was followed later by several hundred thousands of his countrymen who took up their stations around in logging camps and sawmills throughout the country. All of these lads used snuff in its most violent form and as the timber was cut out in the east and the lumber outfits moved west in search of bigger and better trees, the Norsemen went right along with them. Behind they left a trail of empty "snoose" cans a hundred miles wide and an inch deep.

The editor of the New Yorker is apparently laboring under the delusion that there is only one kind of snuff— the kind people sniff up their noses and which cause them to sneeze whole heartedly and with wild abandon. The fact is, there are at least twenty different kinds of

snuff manufactured. Scotch snuff is the kind the editor is thinking of. This is used in the South by the old settlers, some of whom still sniff it. The greater majority of southerners, however, have a little twig of elm, or some such wood, which they chew until the end assumes the general shape of a broom. Then they dip this in a bottle of Scotch snuff and rub it around inside the mouth. When they are through with the stick they put it behind a convenient ear where it rides comfortably until time for the next shot. Very handy and sanitary.

It may interest the editor of the New Yorker to know that there is another kind of snuff manufactured in the United States in such quantities as to be staggering. We have been unable to gather many figures but one year the government collected taxes on 40,655,395 pounds of it.

This kind of snuff is known the country over as Copenhagen, and is the national breakfast food of all Nordic lumber workers, from North Bend, Oregon, to South Bend, Indiana, to say nothing of several hundred thousand Americans and other nationalities who have taken up the habit. It is a concoction of tobacco, salt and attar of roses and is made up in a damp form so that it will stay put when inserted under the lower lip. Damp as it is, the beginner has some trouble in mastering the secret of using it properly.

FALLS CITY SHINGLE MILL on Snoqualmie River, Washington, burning in 1910 after about ten years of operation. (Photo courtesy Mrs. A. F. Coppers)

As a matter of fact, it is something of a thrill—that first chew of Copenhagen. It looks easy to watch an expert insert an educated thumb and two fingers into the little round box and deftly drop a charge into the pocket in his lower lip, which he has been cultivating since early childhood for just this purpose. Beyond a general perking up of the entire system, like a thirsty bum who has just been tossed out of a saloon only to find a forgotten quarter in his pocket, the old timer shows no startling change when the snuff has been tamped home. He brightens up and there is a satisfied gleam in his eye and considerable speeding up of his work around the place, but that's about all. He is used to it and knows just how to handle it.

The beginner watches closely the loading operation and decides to try a "rare" himself. In spite of the fact that the old timer handles a handful of the stuff with no apparent effort, seldom spilling so much as a grain in the transfer from box to lip, the beginner runs up against his first snag right there. Even though Copenhagen is made up damp it has a decided tendency to scatter and stray away from the fold; it insists on wandering from the paths of righteousness and has a habit of disintegrating at the most embarrassing moments. It is not unusual for the beginner to find himself with a small jolt under his lip and the rest of the charge on his chin, floating uncontrolled in and about his tonsils or drifting idly down his shirt collar. It's a habit of snuff.

SHINGLE MILL CIRCA 1902 owned by J. C. Waugh and Ed Freeman near Mt. Vernon, Wash. Teamster John Wylie is man in white hat by horses, the small boy, Guy Freeman. (Photo courtesy John Wylie)

143

COOKHOUSE AT ROBE—Best Shingle Co. This was known as the Tunnel 2 Mill and was operated by Frank Davis near Robe, Wash., from 1906 to 1910. (Darius Kinsey photo courtesy Ray Moore)

WALVILLE'S FAMOUS BLACK CAT was Hoo-Hoo symbol and white man's magic to Japanese green chain gang. Mounted on front end of Walville Lumber Co.'s building, its teeth were clam shells, its whiskers baling wire. At right in photo is Stewart Holbrook who recounts his impressions of the cat in his book "Far Corner." (Photo Stewart H. Holbrook Collection)

However, even the small shot which the tyro manages to pack away in his mouth is enough to afford him the thrill he is seeking. At first he notices only a queer taste and a burning sensation. He can't quite make out what the feeling is other than it tastes like his foot had gone to sleep. It might be the salt; it might be the tobacco, or it may even be the attar of roses, but it doesn't taste like any of them. The burning sensation increases until in a moment or two he loses all sense of taste.

From then on things go round and round. His head swims, his temperature goes up so high that if anyone put a thermometer in his mouth it would explode, the air is full of pin wheels and Roman candles and he had to hold onto things with both hands to keep from floating out the window. Usually when things reach this stage the beginner decides that this is not just the psychological time to learn to use snuff and makes a dive for the drinking fountain. However, one can't smoke around a sawmill and it is only a question of time before he is

SCOTT'S SHINGLE MILL on Burrard Inlet, Vancouver, B.C., about 1908. Eli Buckley is second sawyer from camera in this 12-machine mill. (Photo courtesy Ray Moore)

driven to the expedient of finding a substitute for tobacco, so he tries it again. Each time he finds that the strain is a little easier and before long he is a confirmed user of Swedish dynamite. Then he buys a ten-cent box of it, slips it into his hip pocket and from then on, if deprived of its strengthening influence for even an hour, he is as useless and tired as a blonde manicurist after an American Legion convention.

It is snuff that keeps the big western sawmills and logging camps running. Food and other necessary commodities contribute a certain share to the industry, but Copenhagen snuff is the real force that gets the logs out

of the woods and into the mill. Without it the industry bogs down in the middle like a Dachshund after a full meal and lumber production drops faster than the absent-minded parachute jumper who reached for the ring and pulled the belt out of his pants.

The editor of the New Yorker could get himself lost in a maze of figures on snuff production if he would just start out from the little tip we are about to give him. The city of Bend is one of hundreds of similar lumber manufacturing towns in the Pacific Northwest and its entire population could be comfortably housed in a couple of square blocks of New York's tenement section.

FLOATING COOKHOUSE at Shawnigan Lake, Vancouver Island, B.C., about 1908. (Wilfred Gibson photo from MacMillan and Bloedel, Limited, Collection)

LYTLE'S CAMP in Grays Harbor for loggers and workers in Lytle's Shingle Mill about 1900. (Photo University of Washington)

LYTLE'S SHINGLE MILL—HOQUIAM. (Photo University of Washington)

MORONI SHINGLE CREW Top, left to right—
Charlie Morris, Frank Stein. Middle row—Russell
Clow, Bob Hoyt, Carl Frisk, Buck Clemons, Ray
Hoyt, Harry Johnson, Deyo Russell, Ludwig Han-
son, Joe Briggs, Phil Wylie, Elmer Smith. Front
row—Oliver Helgeson, Carl Hulbert, Bud Jacoby,
Eli Neff, Spike Johnston, Roger Boyd and Ernest
Boyd (father and son now operating Three Rivers
Plywood and Timber Co., Darrington), Clem Fla-
herty, Cassius Bust, Morganthaler. (Darius Kinsey
photo from E. E. Boyd)

We have no intention of trying to figure this out for
ourself. We never were any good at figures, anyway.
All we had in mind was calling the editor's attention to
the fact that the making of snuff in America is still a
leading industry even though the jewelled fingers of the
ladies of the editor's memory are now reaching for
sweeties instead of Scotch snuff. As far as that goes it
is probably only a question of time before the dear girls
take up the Copenhagen habit, anyway.

We feel, however ,that this is not the time to view the
situation with alarm nor even to raise a cry of warning
at the crisis toward which the girls are heading. We
won't be a bit surprised to learn that after trying it the
dear things have decided to give up all bad habits and
retire to a quiet home life, content with their knitting
and alone with their thoughts, with possibly some books
and the family cat for company.

SMALL MILL—TALL STACKS Moroni Shingle
Co., Acme, Wash., started early and produced late
into 1956, owned by E. E. Boyd who came from
Grand Rapids, Wich., in 1903. After working for
Hudson's Bay Co. in Winnipeg and Vancouver, he
operated shingle mills in Sedro Woolley, Turlo,
Alger and Acme. With son Roger A. Boyd, he
started the Three Rivers Plywood and Timber Co.
in Darrington. (Photo courtesy E. E. Boyd)

MILL AT DEMING, WASH-INGTON — 1905 near Mc-Cleary. Shingle mills were usually on pond, river or lake for easiest transportation of logs and bolts. Also water kept wood clean and easier on saws. Brattlie Brothers at Ridgefield taught shingle trade to many who set up own mills. Charles H. White was Brattlie foreman for 24 years. (Photo courtesy C. H. White)

WHITE STAR MILL AFTER FOREST FIRE of 1902. Three shingle weavers wonder what to do now after fire wiped out their jobs and left only twisted iron and ashes. At top, J. J. White, below him his brother Charley. (Photo courtesy C. H. White)

WASHING DOWN CEDAR DUST at Green Tree Saloon near Summit, Wash. On barrel is Charley White, 52 years in shingle mills. Bottom right, second from left —Frank Bagley, next Bill Bailey; extreme right, Billy Van Kirk. (Photo courtesy C. H. White)

WATER LINES
to Mill and Market

SILVERTIP'S RIDE

Where a mighty mountain is held at bay
  By the threat of a brawling stream,
A valley wakes to its toilsome day
  At a sawmill whistle's scream.
Far from salvation, and farther from town,
  By a rutted road, rock-strewn,
A meandering road that winds up and down,
A narrow ribbon of rusty brown,
  Through a wilderness rough-hewn.

From lofty range, over slope and side
  To canyon cleft below;
Like wind-stirred waves of a dark green tide
  Densely the pine woods grow.
Where water wells from a glacier spring
  To the rim of a rock-bound pool,
Rough shacks of a camp to the hillside cling,
While saws and axe made the silence ring,
  And the dawn comes clear and cool.

A ribbon of steel runs from camp to mill,
  Where a Shay makes a daily trip,
With its swaying loads drifting down the hill
  In the leash of the brakeshoe's grip.
But now and again it may chance to be
  An ambulance or a hearse;
Like the night when the boss of the woods and me
Brought down in the engine young Barney McGee
  With a crushed-in hip, and worse.

McGee was a lad who was liked by all,
  But little there was we could do;
With the best of skill the chances were small
  That ever he would pull through.
And hospitals, doctors, nurses and such
  Were a million miles away,
With part of the road in the river's clutch—
A habit it had if we needed it much,
  In the spring when the snow went away.

OREGON LOG FLUMES held out over trucks a long time. The Pengra line was built by enterprising Eugene business men. Northeast of Eugene several flumes ran down to Mariola. Southern Pacific flumed from three big mills, Fischer Lumber Co., 6 miles from Parsons Creek. (Photo University of Oregon)

3-WAY FLUME AT BENE-WAH CREEK in St. Joe National Forest, Idaho. Each line went to a different point and water was diverted as need occurred. Some Idaho flumes had grades up to 12 and 15%. (Photo William Roddy courtesy Chas. H. Scribner)

We knew of another way to town,
  But no one had tried it so far:
The flume! where the timbers go hurtling down
  To their place on a main-line car;
The flume! where the whirling waters sweep
  And foam in their wooden bed,
Whose tenuous trestles span and creep
'Round mountain shoulder and rock-cleft deep
  To smoother reaches ahead.

Twenty miles in a straightaway line,
  And beneath us a mile or so
When the light is clear you may see the shine
  Of the city's reflected glow.
If a man had the guts and could stand the pace,
  The flume is a road to town.
But perilous work he would have to face
On curves and steeps, where the timbers race
  And sometimes shoot over and down.

A few of us talked it over that night.
  But none of us found a way
To help the boy who was making his fight
  With never a word to say.
He was smoking a cigarette to soothe
  The pain and to steady his lip;
We thought his sailing would soon be smooth
But you could not tell if he guessed the truth—
  When in walked Silvertip.

He was a logger of bad repute,
  He gambled, he drank and he swore,
And rumor had it he was a brute
  In a fight, but game to the core.
  A vanquished foe with a humor grim,
  Speaking of grit and of grip,
Once ventured, "A grizzly has nothing on him,"
So, though in build he was slight and slim,
  We had named him "Silvertip."

He stared in a speculative way
  At us and the kid, with a frown;
And in casual manner we heard him say
  He guessed he was off for town.
A wicked joke from a foolish lip,
  Thought every man in that room;
But the boss just scowled at Silvertip,
Then asked, "How in hell will you make the trip?"
  And the answer came back, "By flume."

"I'm kind o' fed up on camp for a while
  And just about due for a fling;
While travel by water was always my style,
  Driving logs on the river in spring;
So if you don't mind I'm off for a spree
  On a bit of raft I built,
But I thought I'd step down here and see
If anyone wanted to share it with me."
  And he smiled to hide his guilt.

150

53 FLUMES IN BRITISH COLUMBIA This Bear Creek line at Adams River, Chase, B.C., was one of the largest. They ranged from a few hundred yards long to the 22 mile flume on the upper Moyie River which bored 300 feet into a mountain. (Photo British Columbia Provincial Archives)

Someone softly swore in the silence that fell,
   But it sounded more like a prayer;
For most of us knew that flume quite well
   And we saw what he meant to dare.
And of course we knew that his play was a blind
   And it didn't deceive us none;
We glimpsed the heart of the man behind
Who would stake his life for one of his kind,
   And smile if he lost or won.

The darkness hid all danger from sight,
   Which was just as well for the kid,
Who was forced to bank on what luck the night
   In its passionless silence hid.
But he rose to his chance with a grim little smile
   Which spoke in a language we knew;
So we picked him to win, for we judged that while
There is many a slip in a turbulent mile
   His partner would bring him through.

We phoned the flume crew and folks below
   To give them what help they might;
And with lantern lit, at the word to go,
   They swept out into the night.
Silvertip, grim in a silent spell,
   Vigilant, keen and bold,
Fearless to face whatever befell,
Sure of his strength and himself as well,
   With a hunch that his luck would hold.

Darkness around them, stark and blind,
   Danger and menace ahead;
Swirl of whitening water behind,
   And the forest aloof and dread.
Ruthless forces forbidding and chill,
   The current in headlong leap
Poised on a brink for a breathless spill,
Swept 'round a curve or flung down a hill
   And whirled through gulches deep.

A light or two adrift in the gloom
   Where voices float out of the night;
Shadowy figures vaguely loom
   And phantom-like vanish from sight.
A hail of cheer is lingering left
   In the speed of a swifter flow
Through yawning blackness of canyon cleft,
'Cross spanning trestles of spidery weft,
   In the grip of a raging foe.

Then luck turned traitor and cunningly wrought
   With chance for a losing throw,
As a hidden projection foully caught
   Their craft with a wicked blow,
Lifted and flung to the brink like a toy.
   Death—and the end—seemed plain,
But Silvertip fought for himself and the boy
With such cunning and might and a fierce wild joy
   That he won them to freedom again.

151

EARLY OREGON FLUMES above—water line to mill at Clatskanie; below—wood flume at Maygar. (Photos Oregon Historical Society)

And now a cabin ablaze and bright
  In the firelight's flicker and play,
With a woman's fingers, tender and light,
  To comfort in woman's own way.
And medical men from the city's best,
  Who promise the boy shall live;
For the grit that held in a cruel test
Will carry him through with such care and rest
  As nature and skill can give.

But Silvertip, though he had nerve and to spare,
  Took refuge in darkness and flight.
He had no hanker for praise or glare,
  So he silently vanished from sight.
He had his fling, like a logger will
  In the days of a red-blooded race;
For the men who work in a camp or mill
Mostly don't show to advantage—until
  There's work for a man to face.

                                        . . . Charles Oluf Olsen

FLUME IN HILLS CREEK AREA. Lewis flume near Dexter, Ore.. extended 8 miles from Lost Creek Valley to railside mill at Pengra where it crossed both state highway and middle fork of Willamette River. (Photo University of Oregon)

WATER LINES TO MILL AND MARKET

Flumes carried water and the romance of lumbering down out of the high places, across gap, gully and swamp, bridging roads and ridges where horse and high lead couldn't reach. Here the big troughs sluiced logs ten and twenty miles to the mills. There sawn lumber floated leisurely and swept around curves so fast it sloshed over the flume rim into canyons below.

There were log and lumber flumes in all the Western states, most of them in Oregon, the longest ones in California. British Columbia used spectacular water chutes ranging from a few hundred yards to a twenty-two mile reach on the Upper Moyie River. This flume, taking logs to the Lumberton mill west of Cranbrook, rode over several trestles 40 and more feet high and at one point bored 300 feet into a mountain. Built in 1920 it was used about ten years.

Another British Columbia flume near Crow's Nest used 25-foot trestles down Alexander Creek. A trough lined with metal connected Phillips Lake with tidewater and one at Cardero Channel was built of galvanized iron. And from Cougar Lake on Princess Royal Island logs rode 1000 feet in a trench cut into solid rock and lined with lumber.

Pine and spruce logs were sluiced out of the woods in a dozen or more places. The Diamond Match Company, operating on the slopes of Mount Spokane, took logs from two widely separated areas, the flumes joining into one just before reaching the mill. Diamond Match had another flume, an 8-mile carry, on Big Creek, Idaho. At one point the grade was almost 15%, averaging 5%. The record says the woods crew ran 6 million feet of logs down this water line to the Priest River. The Potlatch Lumber Company used an 8-mile flume between its Camp T and headquarters near Orofino, dumping logs into the north fork of the Clearwater.

Until the Willamette River flooded and washed out a section, Oregon's Lewis flume probably held a record for variety of crossings. Operated by the Mt. June Flume Company, it ran 8 miles from Lost Creek Valley to the railside mill at Pengra and to serve other mills crossed the state highway and middle fork of the Willamette. Five men maintained the flume in summer, three in winter. One 2-mile stretch was open to the wind and swayed precariously but it took flood water to suspend operations.

The early lumber flumes in the California sugar pine intrigue the imagination. A gigantic flume was originally built in 1875 by the California Lumber Co. from

1800 FEET DOWN TO COLUMBIA GORGE went the Bridal Veil flume carrying "a billion board feet in half a century." Trestles were 100 feet high in some places, the trough 4 feet wide at top, handling stock up to 12"x12"x40'. (Photo University of Oregon)

150 MILLION FEET TO GREENPOINT MILL Log flume of historic Stanley Smith Lumber Co. trip gate flume in Hood River County, Ore. Here rafting dogs have been removed from logs as they bunch up at sluice gate. (Photo courtesy A. A. Lausmann)

its sawmill on the headwaters of the Fresno River to the present site of Madera — a distance of 65 miles. It was taken over after a few years by the Madera Flume and Timber Co. — a great, V-shaped viaduct, 46 inches from rim to rim, each side 36 inches. It cost $300,000 and could float about 250 thousand feet of lumber. It is said to have taken two years to build, that over 5 million feet of lumber went into it, 2100 kegs of nails. To give it buoyancy, the lumber was dried before it entered the water.

A similar flume in the same area was the property of Kings River Lumber Co. Built in the '80s it ran 62 miles from the Kings River mill to the planing mill at Sanger. The width varied from 36 inches at the start to 48 inches near the end and it had about the same capacity as the Madera flume. Lumber went into it bundled about a foot thick, 20 to 28 feet long, the unit held together by iron clamps. About six units were tied together as the trip started. "Flume herders" were stationed about five miles apart along the line and as the flume width increased, they coupled more units together.

"Inspections" were made by boat. A small block of wood, called a "joker" was nailed to a unit of lumber to warn herders an inspection would be coming down. As a rule no trouble was turned up with this kind of inspection.

Both Madera and Kings River were eventually moved so far into mountains and timber, lumber could not be dropped directly into flumes. At the former mill a strap iron tram was built from mill to flume head and at Kings River the carry was accomplished by railroad incline operated by steam hoist.

The Diamond Match Company also had a big spectacular running 45 miles from Lyonsville on the southwestern slopes of Mt. Lassen to the Southern Pacific railside near Red Bluff. "What I recollect clearest about that flume," said Charles O. Olsen who worked in the company camps and walked all the way out on the narrow footboard alongside the flume, "is that it ran through utterly isolated country, away from roads and practically all evidence of life. It circled from crag to crag in the rugged mountain terrain to keep the water back and the lumber from jumping over the side. At times I was dizzily above the ground, then walking flat on it. The flume was V-shaped, about two feet wide at the bottom, five or six feet across the top and maybe four feet deep.

"Midway in the long push I came to the flume tender's station and his kids, several tots, were so scared at the sight of a stranger, they ran like barn cats and hid. The tender got his groceries tied on a parcel of lumber down-flume from Lyonsville, notified of the 'shipment' by telephone. That was some walk." Charley

Olsen was so impressed by this big flume, he wrote the ballad which heads this section — "Silvertip's Ride."

Northeast of Eugene, Oregon, several flumes ran down to Marcola. The Southern Pacific flumed from three big sawmills. Fischer Lumber Company operated a flume 6 miles from Parsons Creek. Wendling was the terminus of another water line — to the L. B. Menefee Lumber Company mill which procured rough stock from other mills by this method. Two other flumes in this area were owned by Mohawk Lumber Company and Brookmayer Lumber Company, the terminus of the latter at Donna.

Booth-Kelly Lumber Company ran a big flume to Saginaw, 3 to 4 feet across the top, 30 feet average above ground. On the bad turns a man stood on foot-wide planks with pike pole to snub the lumber and keep it from jumping out. An old-timer of Eugene is quoted as one of the Booth-Kelly mill men "going out with the lumber on Saturday nights."

"I was a young rooster then. We rode the flume down from Prune Hill where B-K was cutting to Saginaw and caught the Esspee into Eugene. During the week we'd save out good timbers to ride on, 6x8s — 18 feet long made fine 'horses' and we'd balance with a piece of edging. We'd carry our fancy shoes and shirts in sacks on our shoulders. Wore corks, of course — you had to be catty on your feet around some of the curves and steep places. You'd float slow and easy for a while and then it was like water skiing — the timbers would take off like they were going to sail right out of the trough. The flume went under several small bridges. If we felt real frisky we'd jump up on them, run across and jump back on planks again."

Among the men who knew and rode these flumes were — Gene Snellstrom, longtime sawmiller; Frank Graham, an official of Hills Creek Lumber Co. at Jasper. This firm had a flume southeast of Eugene for 25 years. He has said: "We'd ride stringers and make about 5 miles in 45 minutes. It was easy — the trestles were never more than 15 feet above ground."

Also in the Cottage Grove area was the J. H. Chambers line to Dorena, the 8-mile flume of the Woodward Lumber Company from Black Butte to south of Cottage Grove. West of Eugene was the Forcia and Larson line which ran 4 miles west of Noti.

The Bridal Veil Lumber Company flume was famous, extending 1800 feet down the Oregon bluffs into the Columbia River gorge. Fire destroyed the Bridal Veil mill in 1937 and the line was abandoned. H. H. Holland, who was associated with the operation after 1900 with Charles Briggs, estimated the flume took out a billion board feet in half a century.

Trestles were 100 feet high in some places, the flume 4 feet wide at the top, 8 inches at the bottom. It handled stock up to 12x12 — 40 feet long but 8x16 stringers had to be carted down as they would pile up. It sometimes took ten men half a day to break up a lumber jam. The water came out of Bridal Veil Creek and pond, with a feeder spring about halfway. Part of the flow went into 1100-foot penstock, furnishing power for sawmill. It was used nearly all winter.

On the Washington side there was a flume at Borthwick's Landing, below Underwood, another on the Bull Run watershed which ran railroad ties and lumber to Cameron and Hogg's planing mill. The flume at LaCenter dumped ties into the Lewis River. At Camas, the Ledbetters flumed wood to the paper mill.

Lumber flumes in Idaho and Washington were common enough up to 1920. Rawson-Works Lumber Company dropped lumber from its sawmill at Caribel 2000 feet down the mountain by an 8-mile flume to the planing mill across the Clearwater from Kamiah. The Washington Mill Co. had a water line from its Westbranch (Wash.) mill on the Little Spokane to Allen near Milan. This approximate location was later used by the Spokane Lumber Company flume. Seven miles east of Blueslide, Wash., the Wheeler mill ran lumber by water to planers at Blueside. The flume water operated wheel to power the green chain. Gardiner and Powell flumed on Mount Spokane to their planing mill 8 miles down the valley.

One of the few lumber flumes to operate in late years has been the 9-mile water haul from headrig to resaw — of Broughton Lumber Company, Underwood, Wash. Logs are cut into cants at the Willard sawmill and conveyor chains drop them into flume. After an hour's ride they nose up to rolls and are hand fed to resaw.

The Broughton flume was built in 1923 using water of Little White Salmon River. The entire length is supported by trestles, some 80 feet above ground. The upper half slopes gradually, lower half with steep chutes tightly secured to sides of bluff by "deadmen" sunk in rock.

LUMBER FLUME from mill at Sheridan, Oregon. (Photo Oregon Historical Society)

SAWS *and* MEN

THE FILER

Behind the scenes, hid away somewhere
In any old corner there is to spare
The filer is often found
Working with hand, with eye and brain,
So sawyers may have no cause to complain,
In language emphatic and often profane,
Of saws that are timber-bound.

With patience enduring and steady of hand,
A man of worth in the timber land,
He stands in his chosen place.
Carefully gauging and filing each tooth
Keen and bright as the naked truth,
And fit as the eager heart of youth
For its task in a trying race.

Saws are a lot like you and me,
Warped by strain in the same degree,
Grow cranky and worn with age;
They lose their teeth and their tempers, too,
Break under stress, get dull and blue,
And sometimes, as men are apt to do,
Fly to pieces in sudden rage.

Their moods and merits the filer knows;
He cures their faults with crafty blows
And humors the cranky with cunning;
He soothes their troubles and mends their flaws
That they may not fail in the common cause,
For men are but men and saws are saws
And all must be kept in the running.

. . . Charles Oluf Olsen

CEDAR READY FOR CLIMB up log slip, sometimes called jack chain. Cut to length at pond cut-off saw, log is pike-poled into position to be caught by dogs on chain and pulled up to log deck inside mill. (Photo courtesy West Coast Lubermen's Association)

SAWMILL SIGN LANGUAGE

The man with the X-ray eyes, the fellow who uses his head, eyes, both hands and feet to hold his job, has more authority than the chairman of the board. He would use his ears too if that "howling old she cat of a band saw wouldn't make so much noise." He has authority, yes — but he rarely uses it because he's a man of common sense and needs his pay check. And maybe his authority stops short of home.

From the days of little friction drive carriages, top and bottom circular saws, and hand set works, sawyers have had to make signals to the setter to get the kind of lumber the mill superintendent wants. He stands behind a screen or shield, order board at the side of his head, and has to tell the man at the set works where and how to place the log. As the carriage gigs back for another cut, he makes up his mind and holds up his free hand with the first and little finger extended. In fir that's a 6¼" cut.

The sawyer's two levers control feed (he could easily put the carriage right through the end of the mill) and nigger which kicks the next log from deck to carriage. His eyes not only size up the log constantly but take an occasional glance at the behavior of the band saw on the wheel. But it's the hand signal liason between sawyer and setter that raises the grade, mill morale and the sawyer's pay check.

An index finger asks for a 1" cut. Add a thumb and you get 6/4 — six quarter inches or a 1½" cut. All five fingers tell the man with the log to come forward 5". Until saws get silencers, sawyers will be using fingers and are thankful "the old man don't know I got toes."

SAWYER SIGNALS FOR CUT Behind levers and splinter shield, foot controlling log turning device, order board at left of his eyes, head sawyer signals setterman on log carriage for cut. From time immemorial, sawyers and filers have carried on feuds, friendly and otherwise, to prove which "runs" the mill. Both are vital, and with edgerman, can make or break the balance sheet. (Photo courtesy West Coast Lumbermen's Association) (Below) Sawyer signals for 2⅛" cut, next—6¼", (bottom) 4¼" and 6½".

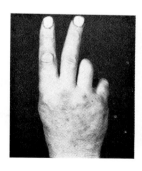 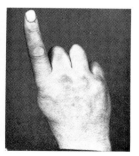 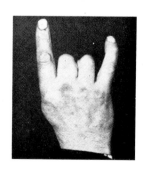

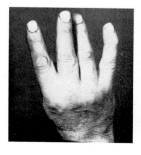 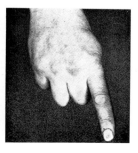 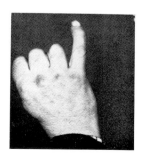

LITTLE ONES OUT OF BIG ONES Gang saw reduces cants to 1 inch boards. (Photo courtesy West Coast Lumbermen's Association)

(Opposite) **SAWYER'S-EYE-VIEW OF DOUBLE CUT BAND** Saw is stopped for cameraman showing teeth on each edge of 14 inch width. Doublecuts require greater handling and sawing skill, more time in filing room, but speed up production since log is being sawed as carriage moves in each direction. (Photo courtesy West Coast Lumbermen's Association)

SAWYERS AND SETTERS
by PAUL HOSMER

longtime editor of Brooks-Scanlon "Pine Echoes" and wry observer of things timberwise.

It has long been an idea of mine that the morale and efficiency of our sawmill crews could be greatly increased through the adoption of a little idea which I have lately thought out all by myself in less than a year. My scheme is guaranteed to do away with the petty jealousies which arise now and then between sawyers and setters and should go a long way toward increasing production by eliminating all the short, but frequent, interruptions and delays which occur so often during the summer when visitors flock to the sawmills to see how lumber is made.

I have noticed that the social standing of sawyers and setters is so indefinite under the present system that every time a young lady visitor comes into the mill the rig loses from one to six minutes while the question of who's who around the place is settled. Being of a sympathetic nature I rather lean towards the sawyer in his noble fight for equal rights in the eyes of our fair visitors. Somebody ought to say something nice about him once in awhile and call attention to the fact that he is really the man who runs the rig. Almost invariably the young ladies who visit our mills during the summer months go away with the impression that the setter is the man who makes the wheels go around, and the setter,

being usually a young man of much pep and vitality, takes advantage of his seat in the sun, so to speak, and does as little as possible to offset this impression. The sawyer, I believe, should be entitled to some credit for his work, but for this reason I venture to broach the subject of uniforms.

Aside from his personal inconspicuousness, the thing that holds the sawyer back the most is the cage in which he works. When a man is set down on the mill floor with a high board fence built around him, a castiron shield on one side, a deck load of logs piled over him and a carriage dashing back and forth in front of him it isn't any wonder that lady visitors fail to pay him proper attention. Only his head and shoulders appear in the public eye at any time, but I contend that if those shoulders were draped in a brilliant red uniform everybody would notice him.

As it is now even the mill foreman forgets about the sawyer in the morning. If the rig is moving and the setter is making strange motions with his fingers he knows the sawyer must be around somewhere and lets it go at that. Now and then the cut inspector, after having made the rounds of the office, the sheds, the planing mill and the yard without finding anything to kick about, filters himself through a maze of belts, live rolls and whatnot down to the sawyer's cage with the firm intention of telling him a few things about cutting up logs. He alone knows that the sawyer is the man responsible for the lumber. After a short but snappy

IN TO GET THEIR TEETH FIXED Automatic gumming and sharpening machine grinds gullets uniformly and buzzes shoulders and points of teeth in same operation. Number and size of saw teeth vary with type of lumber, speed of saw. (Photo courtesy West Coast Lumbermen's Association)

conversation in which a great many naughty words are used, the inspector retires to the deacon seat on the deck with the feeling of a duty well done, and the sawyer, spurred to renewed efforts and brought sharply back to life by this word of warning, bites off another chew and proceeds to run his rig, grade his lumber and tell funny stories to his setter in sign language exactly as he has been doing it for the past ten years and will, no doubt, continue to do for the rest of his life.

There are points about the sawyer which should command attention from an admiring populace, but hidden as he is from the public view, his talents are often wasted. For one thing he is an ambidexterous

individual and it is an education to watch him when he gets under way. Of course, there are other people who can use one hand as well as the other in certain places, such as the lumberjack at dinner time who feeds equally well from either side, but like the pipe organ player, the sawyer not only uses both hands all the time, but both feet as well. After he gets really warmed up to his work it is nothing for him to push the steam feed with one hand, the nigger bar with the other, work all his fingers talking to the setter and use both feet in pressing the doodads in the floor; now and then a real good one will be found who can, in addition to keeping all the above in motion, remove a box of Copenhagen from his

FILERS ARE KEY MEN IN THE MILLS

FILERS WERE KEY MEN IN MILLS (Top left to right) Weyerhaeuser men—Jack Tracey who filed at Longview shingle mill and later at Willapa Harbor; W. J. "Bill" Murphy, Mill 1 Longview, who first filed at Hammond in Garibaldi, Oregon; A. E. "Bert" Proctor, Everett; Harry Armstrong, Mill 3 Longview. (Below left to right) John Sells, filer for English Lumber Co., best known for patenting crosscut saw handle; Bill Proctor, Grays Harbor and Seattle filer and well known band saw expert; Fred Hill, Grays Harbor mills and Ed Bennett, Shevlin-Hixon at Bend, Oregon.

BIG BAND SAWS IN FOR FRESHENING Eighteen-inch bands are mounted in sharpening machines in Manary filing room. Other steps in fitting saws were gumming, swaging, sometimes hammering out kinks, retensioning, "stretching" and brazing ends when saws broke or pieces had to be removed. (Manary Logging Co. photo)

BIG SLAB DROPPED on live rolls as carriage starts forward into another cut. (Photo courtesy West Coast Lumbermen's Association)

left rear pocket, take a chew, mop his brow with a red handkerchief and get his stool out of the rack and under him without missing a lick. When they get this good, however, they are usually retired on a pension and given the title of mill foreman so as to have an excuse for signing the payroll.

The time and place in which the sawyer appears to the worst disadvantage, however, is when visitors to the plant go up on the deck to see the big saws work — especially female visitors. Here it is that the setter is apt to get in a few dirty licks tending to show the gallery that he is somebody and, due to his sensational job on top of the rig, is likely to completely eclipse the sawyer. Invariably the girls ask me if the setter is the man who runs things. If it happens that I am under a financial or other embarrassing obligation to the setter I tell them yes. If, on the other hand, the sawyer is a particular friend of mine I take pains to explain the entire layout and impress on the young lady the fact that while the setter seems to be doing most of the work the sawyer is really the man who tells him what to do.

There seems to be some question of my veracity in the minds of a good many sawyers, however, and just to make sure that I don't make a mistake they are very apt to use methods of their own to correct any misleading impressions which the young lady may seem to be getting. The sawyer knows that the girls cannot be blamed for mistaking a setter for a sawyer. He realizes that to their impressionable minds his setter cuts quite a dashing figure as he swings debonairly back and forth on the darting carriage, but being a man of high intelligence and realizing his power to put a stop to the proceedings any time he wants to, he is usually willing to give the setter a good fair chance to make the dame.

From his commanding position on the carriage, the setter is naturally the first to catch sight of the fair visitor as she comes onto the landing, and this is the signal for him to begin to police up a little and make sure she sees him. He rubs his chin warily and in so doing covertly removes three fingers of snoose which, if found on his person, he fears may count a point against him in her estimation. As the carriage whips back for

the next cut he sways gracefully to the swift motion, dashes his cap recklessly against his knee like a buckaroo at a Fourth of July rodeo, and combs a peck of sawdust out of his hair. With these preliminaries he is ready to strut his stuff.

Awestruck, the young lady visitor is gazing around the mill at the crashing machinery which snaps logs into the air as easily as a man twiddles a match between his fingers, and she does not seem to be paying the proper amount of attention to him which his job demands. Suddenly the setter sits up straight in his seat, yells loudly to the sawyer to stop the rig, pushes every lever on the carriage and, when it stops, lifts himself to his feet. Ah! now she is looking at him. With an air of importance he climbs over half a dozen cylinders and two miles of air hose, meanwhile cautioning the sawyer with a warning hand not to move the rig, and very carefully removes a piece of bark the size of a dollar bill from under one of the dogs. This bark has been in that identical place ever since he came on shift that morning and he knew it would come in handy if he left it there long enough. Then he climbs painstakingly back into his seat, waves a hand airily, grins contentedly and resumes his ride, knowing that the young lady is giving him her full attention.

The sawyer, of course, now wakes up to the fact that something is going on which he doesn't know about, and being an old head at the game, he looks first to the visitor's gallery. Sure enough, just as he thought, there is a girl up there — a good looker, too — and she is watching with an admiring eye the manly form of the young setter who has apparently just saved the sawmill

from serious disaster by removing the piece of bark in time. The sawyer sighs resignedly. He is a man of family and has no interest in the fair visitor, but nevertheless it is going a little too far when a setter deliberately steals the spotlight by running in that old bark gag on him before he has a chance to spot the girl for himself, so he begins to use a little strategy.

Carefully easing the log up to the saw he examines it carefully. Then he backs the rig up to the nigger, whirls the log around three times, pushes it back an inch and immediately orders his setter to set it up again, whereupon he saws off a board. The carriage starts on its return trip so fast that the setter has trouble in regaining his balance, and just as he gets set the rig touches the bumper just hard enough to throw him over the other way. He is rapidly becoming demoralized, and hurriedly setting the log up for the next cut, he is surprised and

JAP SQUARES WERE STAPLE ITEM in '20s. 28"x28" and 30"x30" Douglas fir cants were standard export material to the Orient in the boom days of high mill production. (Photo courtesy West Coast Lumbermen's Association)

somewhat hurt to learn the sawyer signaled for 5|4 instead of 6|4. His dial shows he is not coming out right on the log and he attempts to call the sawyer's attention to this state of affairs, whereupon the latter stops the carriage and with many forcible gestures and a few well chosen words, tells the setter where to head in at. Then, with a casual glance at the gallery which shows him that the young lady is now fully cognizant of his presence, the sawyer majestically takes up his station in the cage and resumes his work. The setter pulls his cap down over his eyes, recklessly takes a fresh shot of Copenhagen in full view of the audience and things go on as before. Some day he will be a sawyer, too, and his time will come.

The idea which I would like to see our sawmill adopt is to give the sawyers a neat but not gaudy jacket of red and gold and a pair of green pants. Of course, he should have a suitable number of epaulets and other insignia to signify his ranking at a glance, the same as any other commanding officer, and the setter should have a uniform of more subdued shade, say gray or olive drab, with a quiet chevron or two — just enough to let him feel his oats, like a corporal. The idea appears sound to me and I would like to see it tried. The sawyer should have a break out of it somewhere.

STIFFS *and* SAVAGES

The mournful chords of "Just A Wearyin' For You" crept out of the black pianola set against the partition that formed the back room. They curled like wraiths around the gaudy-labeled whiskey bottles and pyramids of glassware on the mirrored backbar and settled with an almost audible thud into the big, brass spitoons.

Strong men, who last week were running thousand pound fir slabs down the live rolls or rigging steel on spar trees, dropped salty tears in their nickel schooners of beer.

"Chee-riminey Christmas!" Like a powder blast splitting a log was the voice of the mustachioed bartender. "Light the candles and sing a hymn! Is this a drinkin' joint or a welcomin' party for the new undertaker? Is this town gone and crawled into a bear trap or somethin'? You—Sally! Get off your big hunker and put on a lively roll. Wake up, you mugs settin' there and spend some dough!"

The girl in the red kalsomine bounced the man in the tin pants off the bench and kicked off a glittering shoe on her way to the music box. She flipped the lever and the tearful tones stopped, the perforated paper roll rattling and flapping as it wound to an end. The bartender stomped around the end of the bar and rolled with every step on the pock-marked floor. Behind him came bouncing the husky voice of Eva Tanguay—"I don't care, I don't care—." He hesitated just long enough to slick down his oiled hair and swept wide the swinging doors, bellowing into the street:

"Bank your money here, boys—and have one on the house!"

The Silver Spike Saloon was itself again.

* * *

The Skidroad was at its lustiest between 1895 and 1915. Here was life—everything for the guy with money in his store clothes looking right and left like a hungry hawk for a good time. He was carnal man with a thirst and long deprived of satisfaction of the senses. He was a red-blooded escapee from the woods and some green chain foreman's gibes. He was free and frolicsome and blowing her in was going to be a grand job.

The elbowing and jostling, the bawdy profanity, the roistering and buffoonery—all are parts of this life. With a grin the logger and sawmill stiff dodges a pitch from a job office and another from a bald-headed man in a hand-me-down clothes shop. With the same grin he tosses a half-dollar to an old man mauling a wheezy accordion and singing a quavering ditty. A street vendor with a tray of phony jewelry gets in his way and he nudges him into a female phrenologist making overtures from a doorway on the sidewalk.

In the next block there is more hurly-burly—a drooping peddler of Chinese lottery tickets, the con man with

ALLISON'S RED FRONT SALOON in Tillamook had all the customer conveniences from hand towels to dish of cloves. (Photo Tillamook County Pioneer Museum)

SUNDAY STREET SCENE—1903 Sawmill hands dress up and spend Sunday afternoon in front of Mt. Vernon, Washington, hotel—entertained by fisticuffs and other sports to the accompaniment of violin and guitar. (Photo Stacey Collection, Mt. Vernon)

his sleezy approach, the shoestring beggar, bootblacks and newsies, the street walker, the tin horn, the penny arcade and the female barbers — windows of herbs, teeth and used magazines. A shooting gallery. Back in the planing mill he might think of all these with black misgivings but right now they were his. He made them — so why shouldn't he wade right in?

That was the way this blatant, hilarious, devil-may-care dazzle of The Skidroad lost its wickedness, became only setting for a carouse. They lent tone to the play, as did the tin-panny music pouring through the swinging doors, the clink and rattle of poker chips and dice, the shouts and smell of liquor and wet sawdust. "Try your luck, boys? Bet 'em high and sleep in the streets!"

At night the tempo increased. The extra bartenders polished the mahogany, roulette dealers spun their wheels invitingly, the wheel of fortune man spieled: "Round and round she goes an' where she stops nobody knows!" The swinging doors swung faster and faster. Feet joined feet on the brass rails and if anybody slumped he was carted into the back room or dragged out on the street.

At the curb was the soap-box orator and the Salvation Army troupe with the big up-ended drum — the prayers, songs and exhortations. "Where Is My Wandering Boy Tonight?" The country-bred lassies were selling "War Cries" from saloon to saloon and nobody touched them or made ribald remarks. And the other kind of women inviting molestation. Around any corner — the sporting houses, girlie shows, dance halls and dives for all tempting pleasures. "Come on, honey. Only a lousy dollar. Trip around the world for a pair of 'em."

If The Devil walked down The Skidroad nobody saw him.

PACKERS AT ANACORTES Shingle Co. owned by Vincent and Owen in 1907. Shingles were dropped down chute f r o m sawing floor above, men gathering them into a "packer," making up standard bundles. Strapped, they went to dry kilns. In front is Joe Shransky, behind him Frank Gagnon, in rear Charley White. (Photo courtesy C. H. White)

THIS WAS ERICKSON'S Skidroad view of Portland's famous thirst emporium and rendezvous for working stiffs, adventurers and boomers from the four corners of the world—243 Burnside Street. The bar ran the entire length of the block. (Photo Oregon Historical Society)

ERICKSON'S
by CHARLES OLUF OLSEN

Charles Oluf Olsen has used hammer, anvil and typewriter to fit himself into a niche of logging camp and sawmill memory. Born in Denmark, he short-staked himself in and out of every state for over fifty years. By trade he has been a blacksmith but by inclination a writer and his output has covered the West Coast woods. With a mind as keen as an axe blade and a facile writing style which he acquired after he learned English at the age of fifty, Charley Olsen is full of fun yet solemn as a sphinx. In verse and article he has always accented the viewpoint of the working stiff with a fierce love for his fellow man.

It is a long look back to the nineties. Most of the men who then knew August Erickson are now grizzled old-timers. Lonesome figures of yesterday, these think of the man who passed away on a prisoner's cot in the Good Samaritan hospital during the month, and another day rises vividly in their minds. They see what was almost another civilization. They feel the wild pioneering days of their youth.

The manner of Erickson's passing revived the glamor that clung around his name. It enhanced the fame of this picturesque ruler of his little world, this stage king who played his hour within the four walls of his world-renowned saloon at Second and Burnside streets, Portland. The tragedy of his death must have set men all over the world to talking. His fame, in song and story, reached even to those far-off, out-of-the-way places where only rovers go.

Erickson, like many a gambler before him, played a losing hand to the bitter finish. He sat at the last facing heavy odds, in an unfamiliar game. He miscalculated his hand. He made foolish bets. The percentage against him ate up his stake and ill health blurred his judgment, until at last Death put the cards away.

The men who crowded his massive, mirrored bars are scattered to the winds. Loggers and ranchers, railroad men and miners, fishermen and sailors, prospectors, cowboys, stakey men and stiffs; high and low, adventurers all, they came from everywhere, drawn to his corner as iron filings to a magnet.

For Erickson's was more than a drinking-place; it was a wide world's rendezvous. Had you lost track of a pal, like as not you would find him waiting for you there, his elbow on the bar, a huge, frothy scoop of beer in front of him. Sought you some particular man, you would in time see him pass in the throng that milled in and out through the swinging doors. The whole world of roving labor passed here in review. Life lay lightly on the shoulders of this crew who frolicked before the

VENEER WAS PEELED ON 40 INCH LATHE and sheet was split on center in this early day Washington plywood mill. (Photo Ames Collection, University of Washington)

attentive barkeepers, made eager groups around the gambling tables, talked in loud, assertive voices, sang the songs of a dozen tongues or, elbow to elbow, lined the bars drinking, arguing, listening to the music or boasting of their exploits. They were largely workers, doing the hard, manual labor of the frontiers, on a temporary spree of enjoyment and making the most of it while money and time were theirs. It was in such coin they paid themselves for months of enforced abstinence from social excitement, taking revenge for weary days of drudgery. Drinking their fill of pleasure to last them till the next period of indulgence.

But Erickson's was no blessed asylum for bums. Fellows of that stamp got scanty sympathy there. I recall a sunny spring morning some thirty years ago: After a big schooner of beer and a short but spirited attack on the free-lunch counter under the watchful eye of the porter, I passed outside and stood loafing in front of the entrance, soaking in the warmth. I had just come down from Seattle. The logging camps were opening, but jobs as yet were scarce and my pennies were disappearing. As I lingered there, figuring on my next move, a burly cop rounded the corner and in a casual, business-

like way grabbed my hand, turned it over and scrutinized the palm. With a non-committal grunt he dropped it and went on. I turned to a fellow who had been watching this performance from inside the saloon and asked:

"What in the world did the cop do that for?"

"Oh," came the answer, "harness-bulls in this burg has their instruction; around this corner here they frisk a bo to see if he's got calluses on his paws; if he ain't it's the rock-pile for him, savvy." Then he added scornfully: "You kin get calluses from glomming the rods on a rattler; these cops don't know it all!"

Not that Erickson's place wasn't generous. If you had "blowed" your pile there you might depend on a lift to get you a job or perhaps your fare to reach it. But everybody could not be helped. There must have been an appalling number of askers and it was imperative that rules should be established, a limit set. Begging was the one unforgivable offense. Stewbums, pan-handlers, moochers and spearers of drinks were given the short shrift of the bum's rush, if not a policeman's arms!

When gambling was outlawed, when Fritz and Blazier left Erickson and opened bars of their own across the street and took some of his trade with them; when the

VENEER CLIPPER IN EARLY DOOR FACTORY (Darius Kinsey photo from Jesse E. Ebert Collection)

lid was clamped on the town in crusades on vice, the red-light districts eliminated and the lurid attractions of that section began to fade, the character of Erickson's customers changed and with them many of the old ways. The gambling games dwindled to petty stud-poker in the back rooms; the splurging of the revellers in the place gradually ceased and the premises often had but a sprinkling of patrons where before there had been crowds.

The drinking in Erickson's was of the hectic, impulsive kind; it differed altogether from the quiet places uptown where little noise was tolerated and polite, conventional manners ruled. Here on Second and Burnside the boisterous and hearty, but often rude, spontaneity of rough men had free rein. A spender usually invited the bartender, those who happened to be already lined up, all within reach of his voice, or even the whole house to have a drink at his expense. His inclusiveness or exclusiveness depended on the size of his stake and the generosity of his spirit. A man seldom drank alone, especially in the evening, unless he was down to bed-rock. "Come on, all you fellows, and have something," was the slogan there. An invitation to share someone's spree would not be long in coming after you had entered Erickson's. It was the spirit of the place and the day.

The gambling was also of the plunging, reckless kind. It was in the evening that this sport was in full sway. Portland itself contributed a very small portion to the professional gamblers' income. The bulk of it came from the woolly sheep that flocked in from the woods, the grading camps, ranches and mines. These supplied the fleece that kept the spoilers in comfort for a large part of the year. Fourth of July and the Christmas holidays were their banner times; then the wool was heaviest and easiest to shear. The workingmen of the frontier were for the most part heedless, generous players and easy losers. For most of them this was a blessing in disguise. Far better to go broke in one glorious, meteoric orgy of a single night than to squander your stake on a continuous drunken blow-out of three weeks' duration. Better king for an hour and then back to drudgery, with wild glory booming in your ears, than never to have tasted life's brimming cup.

Naturally, the deplorable vice that thrives on the outskirts of districts like the North End was in full evidence here. Nor was it camouflaged. It flaunted openly, barring the periods following the occasional crusades that public opinion called for. It was an accepted custom of the times, connived at by the police powers, considered a necessary evil, an indispensable adjunct to a really "swell" time as demanded by the money-spenders who might otherwise have transferred their coin and their desires to a more "wide open" town.

Looking back over the intervening dry years to those flaming days, what is the old-timers' judgment of them? They were both good and bad. I often wonder now just what it was that impelled men to stand bellied against a bar all night long, downing drink upon drink long after thirst and desire had fled squandering a stake acquired by the most brutal, manual labor, often earned literally in sweat and blood. From these calmer, more disciplined days it appears like sheer madness. That a man should come to Erickson's, step to the bar, throw his stake on it, turn around and bawl out: "All you stiffs come and have something," and stay there guzzling until it was gone, when the earning of it had actually been a case of "A hundred days for a hundred dollars" seems as foolish as impossible. But it was so.

Maybe the times were to blame. Spending one's stake was then a universal and respected pastime, encouraged not alone by the profiting saloon-keepers, but often by the bosses on the job. A stakey man was apt to be independent and a hungry belly always guaranteed a willing pair of hands, at least until its wrinkles had disappeared. The men who drank in Erickson's were a husky, hard-working lot, for the most part young and spirited. Cooped up for months in places as devoid of pastimes as a prison-cell and then suddenly let loose in a world of pleasures, theirs for the demanding as long as they had the price, they satisfied their desire for play in the same direct, brutal way in which they conquered their tough jobs. Tough times and tough men!

The attraction of Erickson's for these men was the comradely, democratic atmosphere, the cheerful setting, the hilarious and carefree companionship, the devil-may-care spirit. Even if there was the morning after, of furred tongues and aching heads, they were willing to pay the price — it was well worth it.

But lest we forget: There were also those who, clear-eyed, red-checked and bright-minded, lined up at the bar and stayed there until they were carried away, hours later, to a back room, where they lay on the floor dead drunk — broke, corpse-like, repulsive. Erickson's had no monopoly of these things; they were the regular outcropping of the saloon of that day.

Years lend enchantment to those joys. I remember the delicious concoctions Erickson's accomplished bartenders could conjure from the mysterious-looking bottles on the back bar — bottles that teased my imagination with their odd shapes, suggestive labels, queer, fantastic names and attractive colors. That old-time Manhattan cocktail with its genuine marachino cherry on a toothpick and an ensnaring perfume! On frosty mornings there was a cer-tain chill-chaser at the making of which one of the drink-dispensers was a wizard; a thin glass, delicate almost, half full of boiling water, a silver teaspoon of powdered sugar, a generous dollup of gurgling, amber-colored Jamaica rum, a touch of lemon peel and the merest dash of nutmeg, made a drink that was 100% efficient, stimulating and intoxicating, a drink that would have thawed out Paul Bunyan in the memorable Winter of the Blue Snow! And who could forget on Christmas holidays the bowl of Tom and Jerry? The golden sheen of the jolly, frothy mixture that mellowed your mood, put blarney on your tongue, enraptured your senses and enthralled your spirit, until the whole world was truly a place of good will toward men!

And let us not pass by the toothsome free lunches. Everything savory — and salty — on display to entice the patron to eat, but nicely calculated also to make him drink! Fish of all kinds from strange parts of the globe, catering to outlandish tastes; a regular delicatessen where everything was "free gratis" — provided you kept drinking. Meat balls, fish balls and "balls that were no balls at all," as the ballad had it. My mouth waters when recollection flies back to the steamed clams and broth, the stews, the soups and all that array of tempting dishes!

They are all gone now.

A ghost-like place now, is Erickson's, teeming with memories. What stories those bars could tell! Here men related wonderful tales of prowess on land and sea; many a perilous voyage was sailed around those mahogany counters, many a hazardous trail traveled again, many a daring feat of valor reenacted! Safe to say more logging was done within those walls than in all the woods of the Northwest since logging began!

Free from the greatest of faults, commonplaceness, it breathed the tang of the sea, the scent of forests, the smell of sage-brush desert. Here was the flavor of the wilds, the spirit of untamed things. Erickson's belongs to the Northwest's youth, its period of wild-oats sowing. It but expressed the times. It was a reckless age, a prodigal age, a mad age, if you will, but who will deny that it was an age worth while?

MILL AND CREW ON YUKON Roy Rutherford grew up in Falls City, Washington, started saw-milling at Valdez in 1901, mushed over the trail to Fairbanks in 1904. Independent Lumber Co., above, a Rutherford operation, was sold to S. Widman in 1912. (Photo courtesy Roy Rutherford)

SKIDDING WATER FOR BOILERS Mt. Vernon pioneer, John Wylie (foreground) hauled water for sawmills with this 10-horse team. He came from Michigan in '98 after oxen had logged, worked in sawmill at Clearbrook, Whatcom County, then for many years drove teams in woods. He hauled shingle bolts over planked roads for Green and Hammer mill at Skyu Slough (now Skytopia) and for mills pictured opposite. This photo taken by early Mt. Vernon photographer Robertson in 1903 on Bay View Ridge, site of present airport. Man by rear barrels is Dick White, next Linberg and George Hobson. (Photo courtesy John Wylie)

"FREE FARE TO HAPPY VALLEY"

Call them "job sharks," "slave shops," "workhouse traps" or whatever you will, the employment offices that funneled men off the Skidroad and into mills and woods had a timely worth, however misused or misunderstood it was.

You saw the job boards at dozens of places along Vancouver's Cordova Street, San Francisco's Embarcadero, Portland's Burnside and Seattle's Occidental — blackboards or boards painted black vying for attention with the saloon, tattoo parlor or honky tonk. You were looking for them with one eye and avoiding them with the other. It was just that you sort of wanted to know where you might be going after you got off this job of getting yourself a good time. But you didn't want to get too chummy with those ominous white chalk marks:

CHOKER STR $3.50

2 AXE MEN FAIRHAVEN $3

STACKER — MILL CITY

DOGGER — PIE MEN — TAIL SAWYER

WE GIVE YOU THE BEST DEAL IN TOWN

No matter what the sign said it all meant work and you couldn't get too giddy about it. "Say, mister, I worked there at Hokum City and I don't go back. I'll go for the green chain 'cause me, I'm scared of saws and anyway I like fresh air and rain. Man, do I like rain. Pond man? Hunh-unh. No two-stepping on them slip-pery logs. Say — I just remembered. I don't want no job. Remembered a guy that owes me a ten spot. See you tomorrow maybe."

So employment offices had a function. Mills and camps needed men constantly and every day thousands had to go back to work. The job offices were necessary to the boom conditions of lumbering, a natural outgrowth of good times.

Back in the early days when the first West Coast mills were getting started, men met in the general stores and exchanged news about jobs, and the storekeepers, in touch with the general situation, grew to be employment agents of a sort. But in those days labor turnover was at a minimum. A man didn't just up and quit a good sawmill or woods job. He had to have a driving urge to leave a camp or mill and hike miles over a rough, muddy trail with a bed on his back, carrying his own food and cooking pots.

The steam sawmill, with both California and Yukon gold rushes, changed the pattern. The steam mill was a bigger operation, needed a permanent location, not only for the boiler and engine but for machinery to dress, plane, groove and dry lumber. It took a bigger crew to run it and so began to have a continuing employment problem.

Men were so scarce in Portland when Oregon's first steam sawmill was built there, not enough manpower could be rounded up to put the 16-inch square hewn

timbers for the framework into place. A flat-boat was sent to Oregon City for men and came back empty. The beams were finally hoisted into place with a block and tackle on a homemade derrick. When men still stayed away, convicts from Oregon State Penitentiary were put to work.

This sort of condition was bound to right itself and up sprang American ingenuity in the form of job-getters. These employment offices sent appeals to the cut-out areas of Michigan, Minnesota and Wisconsin to recruit men for woods and mill jobs and as trains and ships brought them out, they went right to work and sent back home for their brothers and cousins.

Most employment offices in lumbering's heyday were two-way establishments, even those run by saloon keepers in their spare time. A man getting a job through the agent was entitled to store his bedding and belongings free of charge until he shipped out. While he was gone he could have his mail sent there and meet his friends at this spot when he came back in town. Now, if his particular kind of a job wasn't on the board, he could lay down a five dollar bill with some information as to how to reach him while he was having his good time.

Bed rolls and personal belongings were placed in a "bin" in the back room — an enclosure made of slats and chicken wire with a padlocked door. After the "turkey" was cashed it was sure to be buggy because those

pests in a blanket or two would run rampant through the whole lot.

As a rule employment offices were what you expected them to be. They looked at employers and worker customers with an honest eye. They dealt fairly with both parties, supplying the best labor obtainable and at times advancing rail fare to the job to men who looked trustworthy. But there was naturally a minority who didn't care to whom or where they shipped men as long as they got their fees. Among these "jobs sharks" were those whose specialty was "free fare," meaning they sent men

HARDLY EVER SEE THIS NO MORE Douglas fir planks like these would be worth a king's ransom today—No. 1 clear, 3¼"x4'x16'. (Darius Kinsey photo from West Coast Lumbermen's Association)

to employers known to be unfair.

One thing only was required of "free fare" rides — bedding. Since many of them were "mill inspectors" who didn't aim to work, only wanted transportation to some "happy valley" where life might be easier but probably wasn't, they were not packing more than they could get in their stomachs and pockets. So they had to hustle a bed roll. The second-hand stores were sharp to this and would sell you something like a roll for a dollar or so. The outside of this bargain looked genuine if considerably bunk worn, but inside it was stuffed with newspapers, rags or maybe a brick. If the "free fare" boys arrived at the sawmill or logging camp at night, they handed over their bed rolls as security for a bunk, supper and breakfast. If they arrived during the day, they just walked away — period.

Few of these men worked at their jobs — a week or ten days at the most — then moved on in the same manner to another spot. Mills that resorted to "free fare" practices had standing orders with employment agencies to send a given number of men at stated intervals. This was called the three-crew system — one crew quitting, one working, one on the way to work. "Free fare" employers

naturally accumulated store rooms full of turkeys and periodically hauled them out into the air with pike poles and gave them the kerosene and match treatment.

There was a type of labor agent who specialized in supplying Japanese and other ignorant aliens to sawmills badly in need of men. Some of these agents used legitimate enough methods but many were unscrupulous and exploited the laborers for their own gain. One practice was to send aliens to nearby mills so that close contact could be maintained. Then each week or oftener the labor agent would go personally to the mill and collect the exhorbitant wage percentage he claimed was due. Often he would organize dice games and use other ruses to fleece the workers and keep them dependent on his services. There is at least one case on record where rebellious Japanese turned on the job shark with knives and in the resulting melee, six of them were shot to death.

It is safe to assume it was not this employment man who, during the downfall of the Spanish monarchy, chalked up this immortal message on his skidroad bulletin board:

WANTED — NEW KING FOR SPAIN
NO BLANKET NEEDED